HEART OF SOUL

The Lauryn Hill Story

By Elina and Leah Furman
Published by Ballantine Books:

THE HEAT IS ON: 98°
HEART OF SOUL: The Lauryn Hill Story

HEART OF SOUL

The Lauryn Hill Story

Elina and Leah Furman

BALLANTINE BOOKS • NEW YORK

A Ballantine Book
Published by The Ballantine Publishing Group
Copyright © 1999 by Elina and Leah Furman
Cover photo © Albert Ferreira/Globe Photos, Inc.

All rights reserved under International and Pan-American Copyright Conventions. Published in the United States by The Ballantine Publishing Group, a division of Random House, Inc., New York, and simultaneously in Canada by Random House of Canada Limited, Toronto.

Ballantine and colophon are registered trademarks of Random House, Inc.

www.randomhouse.com/BB/

Library of Congress Catalog Card Number: 99-90830

ISBN 0-345-43588-5

Manufactured in the United States of America

First Edition: November 1999

10 9 8 7 6 5 4 3 2 1

For our mom

Acknowledgments

Thank you, Cathy Repetti, for giving us the opportunity to explore the life and times of this tremendous young artist. Thanks also to Betsy Flagler for all her work on this manuscript. As always, Giles Anderson deserves more gratitude than words can ever express. Nikkah's enthusiasm was as great an inspiration as ever. And finally, for supporting us, putting up with us, and making everything worthwhile, thanks, Mom.

Too Good to Be True

As the reigning empress of hip-hop music and culture, Lauryn Hill needs no introduction. Who, after all, is not aware that this twenty-three-year-old songstress has broken all records by winning ten Grammy nominations and taking home five Grammy awards? Is there any confusion as to what record-setting rap trio spawned her arrival on the music scene? Can anyone truly say that he or she has never heard a single word of praise for the artist that every celebrity and their unknown cousins have been talking about for the past year? Thanks to the media's gimlet-eyed coverage, most people have been well educated on the woman behind *The Miseducation of Lauryn Hill*.

Ever since she was a child living in South Orange, New Jersey, Lauryn was pegged as the girl who would be queen. With brains, beauty, confidence, and a strong connection to God, she was known as the most talented young woman for miles around. Before her voice made her a star,

1

it was Lauryn's acting skills that set the creative community on its ear. By sixteen, she was already a regular actress on a daytime soap. By eightteen, she had added two movies to her résumé. All the while, Lauryn was the ornate centerpiece of the Fugees, playing clubs and making music in every spare moment of her jam-packed itinerary.

Cut to 1998. Lauryn is at the center of the music industry. Her solo album is hailed as the decade's supreme achievement. Rap, reggae, R&B, soul—Lauryn sees no boundaries. She expertly blends the smooth grooves of jamming oldies with the strident rhythms of the spoken word. In full control of her vision and her art, the young woman shocks the music world by writing, arranging, and producing her own album.

With no end of accomplishments to her ubiquitous name, Lauryn has come to symbolize the essence of feminine strength and the power of the human spirit. Her acceptance of the Grammy for Best New Artist was classic Lauryn Hill. After Eric Clapton and B. B. King announced her name, she walked to the stage as if in a daze while the packed Shrine Auditorium reverberated with jubilant applause. Dressed in the height of hip-hop fashion—an easy sarong skirt, a decidedly understated white tank top, and an oversize red knit beret—and holding a miniature brown volume in her hand,

Lauryn proceeded to warn the audience that what she was about to do was "a little bit different for the Grammys."

A hush fell over the crowd as she opened her tiny book and read the beginning of Psalm 40. With her few vociferous detractors—and even her countless rhapsodic admirers—all given cause to comment upon the sermonizing tone of her debut solo album, a Bible reading at this juncture brought Lauryn dangerously close to being branded a latter-day Crusader. Yet somehow she managed to avoid the label. After reciting a line from the psalm, "He put a new song in my mouth, a hymn of praise to my God, many will see and feel and put their trust in the Lord," Lauryn didn't ramble. She thanked her family, her colleagues, and her children for "not spilling anything on Mommy's outfit."

Such beguiling directness at every turn proves that there's nothing sanctimonious about Lauryn Hill. Her every word and gesture emanates straight from the heart, leaving the public with no room for doubt as to her authenticity. Her spirituality and wisdom, so evident in the lyrics of her songs, come from hard-won experience. Do not be fooled by her young age and sweeping success; Lauryn has had to struggle to receive the credit that's been her due for years.

As a woman in the male-dominated entertainment industry, she has overcome the unyielding undercurrent of opposition from the old-boy network. As an unmarried mother-to-be, she twice took a leap of faith and refused to bow down to the many friends and onlookers who heaped censure upon her decision to keep her babies. As an African American, she actively sought out the role models who could guide her toward the realization of her greatest dreams. And as an artist in today's result-oriented music business, Lauryn looked to God for the strength to experiment.

If the genre-defying contents of her solo CD are any indication, then Lauryn truly is playing with a full deck. While she openly credits divine Providence for her inspiration, *The Miseducation of Lauryn Hill* is itself a symbol of gratitude to heaven above. Looking beyond the almighty dollar, Lauryn has eschewed the hit-generating formula she knows so well to aim for a goal far loftier—artistic and personal integrity. The result is an album poised on the razor's edge between old-school soul and the future of mainstream music. By fusing hip-hop with the music of her childhood—reggae, soul, and R&B—she has revealed previously unseen vistas to thousands of aspiring musicians.

Loaded with positive messages, the album follows her development from a naive youth to the maverick she is today. Unfolding through verses, it tells Lauryn's autobiographical tale. While *Miseducation* is her own version of an American quilt, the events of Lauryn's life are all the more interesting for their role in informing her art. Passing through blissful innocence to worldly sophistication, she has fought her way back to spiritual peace after watching all her illusions shatter. In so doing, Lauryn Hill has at last reclaimed the happiness that is her birthright.

Chapter One

Looking Back

No story is without its preamble. Lauryn Hill's cultural and musical roots preceded her birth by decades. When she first discovered the soothing power of music, Lauryn had round, chubby cheeks and tight Pippi Longstocking braids plaited by her mother's hand. In fact, she still had to stand on tiptoe and reach with all her might just to open the bathroom mirror cabinet. She was only six years old at the time, but her records were considerably older. "I would go into the basement and take my little carry-all record player," she told the *Illinois Entertainer*. "I listened to all those 45s, some of which still had my mother's maiden name on them! It was classic soul from the 60's and 70's."

Young Lauryn's beloved soul and R&B performers—such as Curtis Mayfield, Roberta Flack, Marvin Gaye, Nina Simone, Stevie Wonder, and Aretha Franklin—were themselves the scions of blues and jazz greats like Billie Holiday, Louis Armstrong, and Lena Horne. In the sixties, soul-imbued music reached critical mass with the Stax and Motown record labels actively pursuing new talent, grooming them for greatness, and then releasing what seemed to be an endless supply of hits.

Soul music showed no sign of loosening its grip on Billboard's Hot 100, and the nation's youth had a wide variety of artists from which to choose when compiling their record collections. Lauryn's mother, Valerie, was one of the many teens who chose to turn her petty cash into vinyl. "I amassed a nice little pile—stacks and stacks of Motown, Philly International, Stax, Marvin, Stevie, Aretha, Donny Hathaway, Gladys Knight—that whole thing," she told *Rolling Stone*.

While the fifties had seen Chuck Berry introduce the world to R&B's randy brother, rock 'n' roll, it was not until the white musicians adopted the genre in the late sixties and early seventies that rock became a crossover success story. Yet even when all eyes and ears were focused on the Beatles, the Rolling Stones, and Jimi Hendrix, Motown Records' enduring success showed that R&B remained a powerful contender in the battle for record buyers' attention.

Variations on the sounds of rock and soul would come into the mainstream with the funky stylings of James Brown, Sly and the Family Stone, and Prince, but the tide of hip-hop would not swell until the mid-eighties.

Although Lauryn would take to it instantly, she would never forget or deny the classic soul music that had already found a permanent place in her heart.

Born in South Orange, New Jersey, on May 25, 1975, Lauryn was by no means a child of the privileged class. Although her parents, Mal and Valerie Hill, were hardworking middle-class denizens of the Newark suburb with little money to spend on designer clothes and fancy schools for their children, she grew up with all the advantages enjoyed by the society's upper crust, and then some. "I wasn't raised rich," she told *Essence* magazine. "But I never really wanted the things that we didn't have. I think my parents instilled in us that we didn't need lavish things. As long as we had love and protection, we were always taken care of."

Lauryn's father and mother, a computer analyst and a high school English teacher, respectively, had nothing but love for their kids. Often sacrificing their own wishes for the benefit of their children, they raised Lauryn and her brother, Malaney, to appreciate their many blessings. As a result, the two never had cause to focus on the greener pastures that were the domain of some of their peers. Even the television ads that promised instant gratification via Snoopy Sno-Cone Machines and Betty

8

Crocker Easy-Bake Ovens held little allure for the contented youngsters.

The Hills' efforts to nourish the talents of their offspring were considerable. Malaney, three years Lauryn's senior, had all the musical instruction one boy could handle. Playing the sax, drums, and guitar, he had the musical education a child of the upper class might envy.

Lauryn, likewise, was not musically deprived while growing up. Her parents soon realized that to deny their daughter musical training would be tantamount to grand larceny. Lauryn had a gift, and as good parents they saw to it that she did not squander her talents. "Her violin teacher kept telling us, 'I don't believe how musical she is,' " said Valerie. "She just had this effect on people who listened to her."

Aside from the records that were soon to influence Lauryn, it was her parents' own musical inclinations that set the stage for the would-be superstar. After all, nurture can only do so much; for everything else there is genetics. Mal Hill's voice is no doubt partially responsible for the talent that's now got the nation's feet tapping to one beat. While his high tech day job belies the fact, Mal was quite the crooner in his day.

Before settling down to raise the family, Lauryn's father sang in nightclubs. Later, he kept his vocals in tune by serenading newly-weds at weddings. But that wasn't all he did.

"My father is the type of father who at a wedding would try to break-dance and embarrass us—he was that cat," Lauryn fondly recalled in *Entertainment Weekly*.

While Valerie enjoyed playing piano, and even tried teaching her daughter how to play, her verbal aptitude was her real gift to Lauryn. Valerie's communication skills brought her only a modest income as an English teacher, but they did wonders for her daughter, who would one day bring self-expression to a whole new level.

"My mother always thought I'd be a star," Lauryn sings on "Every Ghetto, Every City." Looking at her now, it's easy to see why. Of course, as a child, she also had je ne sais quoi to spare. An entertainer through and through, Lauryn always took the lead in planning events for her circle of friends. "I was real crazy and always like 'Lets put on a show!' " she told *Rolling Stone*. "Always singing and dancing—everything I did was dramatic. I was wild."

Other kids were quick to follow little Lauryn's lead and join in her games. The obeisance she inspired in her young contemporaries may have had something to do with the distinctive quality of her voice. "I was an old lady since kindergarten," she told MTV. "It's the voice. It's the deep, low voice. All the little girls used to be like, [raises her voice to falsetto] 'Hi, I'm Sue.

10

I'm Kelly.' And I used to be like, [drops two octaves] 'Hey, what's up, how you doin'? I'm Lauryn.' So, I've always sort of been a little bit older."

Lauryn's enthusiasm for the performing arts communicated itself to her friends, her teachers, and her family. Valerie and Mal encouraged their daughter to pursue her interests in music, dance, and acting. But the more conventional professions were also held in high regard by the Hill clan. Since she loved her "very, very cool" parents, their emphasis on education rubbed off on Lauryn. "When I was a very little girl," she told *Harper's Bazaar*, "I wanted to be a superstar-slash-lawyer-slash-doctor. I had an agenda."

With Lauryn around, there was never a dull moment in the Hill household. Her attempts to show off for her family were always met with positive reinforcement, and she loved the attention that came with being in the limelight. Valerie simply doted on her younger child; she told *Teen People* that "she did lots of things that kept us entertained."

However, Lauryn's love of performance did not begin and end with the presence of an audience. Always resourceful, Lauryn could while away the hours whether she was surrounded by her admirers or spending time by herself. Even when her brother was out playing with the neighborhood boys, and her parents were too busy to pay her much mind, she was never at a loss for activity.

With her toys, Lauryn would often orchestrate her own musical theater. Since time passed virtually unnoticed while she was thus engaged, she grew to love the singing and acting irrespective of the praise that they so often evoked. "I would come home from teaching and she'd sit on the floor by my bed while I was taking a nap, and she would create her own play with her dolls and toys. She could do that for maybe an hour. She would sing to them, she would talk to them," recalled Valerie.

One day, Valerie took her daughter to see the movie that all the little girls were talking about—*Annie.* Lauryn watched the singing and dancing with an interest that went beyond a mere child's wonder. She was no more than seven years old, but even then she knew that she wanted to be the one singing "Tomorrow" and tap-dancing on the steps of the Warbucks mansion with Albert Finney. After the movie, Valerie remembered in *Essence,* "Lauryn asked if there could ever be a black Annie."

If Lauryn's present confidence is any indication, her mother's response must have been something along the lines of "If there can be a black Dorothy, sure there can be a black Annie." Raised to believe that anything is possible, Lauryn set her sights high. She had so many wide-ranging goals, one hardly knew what her

The Lauryn Hill Story

field would be. Nonetheless, everyone was certain that whatever road she chose, distinction would follow.

Creative children, as a group, aren't known to excel in scholastics. Yet, even with Lauryn's formidable academic record, everyone who knew her felt that music was her true calling. It all began when, as a mere wisp of a girl, she wandered into her family's basement and found a gold mine—her mother's old record collection. "They all came upstairs. And thus began a journey," Valerie told *Rolling Stone*. "She started to play that music and loved it. One o'clock in the morning, you'd go in her room and you'd see her fast asleep with the earphones on. The Sixties soul that I'd collected just seeped into her veins."

One of the first records she listened to was *Santana: Abraxas,* an album that predated her birth by some five years. In *Vibe*, she remembered the day of her formal introduction to music vividly: "I was fooling around in the basement one day, I think I was six or seven years old, and I found a 45. I didn't have any records at the time, and I thought it was the most beautiful thing I ever heard."

From that moment on, Lauryn was like a kid with a brand-new toy. Except, for her, the thrill didn't wear off with the novelty. "There was something sacred about those old records," she

13

told *Entertainment Weekly*. "They meant so much to me, and they . . . had a lot to do with the soundtrack of my life."

In the first few years of the eighties, pop music was being swallowed up by the synthesizer. Computers were responsible for much of what the public would hear on the radio, but Lauryn marched to the beat of a different drum. She preferred the human quality of her mother's soul records to the smoothed-out edge of popular music. After hip-hop finally hit the scene, Lauryn would join her friends in rapping its praises, but up until that time she was content to listen to the golden oldies with her parents, grandparents, aunts, and uncles. "I'd be the kid at family barbecues in the middle of Newark listenin' to the oldies station with the old folks," she remembered. "They'd go, 'Oh, that's Blue Magic!' And I'd go, 'No, it's the Chi-Lites.' "

Amazingly, Lauryn knew just about all there was to know about the history of soul by the time she was eight. Her knowledge was more a testament to her ability to connect with the music on an emotional level than to her memory skills. It was this connection that inspired her to raise her own voice in song whenever the chance arose. To this end, Lauryn formed a vocal group with her childhood friends. "We had so many names I don't remember them all," she told *Vibe*. "I was always very dramatic. I was very ridiculous. You know when you're just happy to sing?"

Valerie took note of her daughter's musical bent. And even as she diligently tracked Lauryn's schoolwork, she "always felt that [Lauryn] would somehow, some way be involved in music."

The lengths to which Lauryn Hill presently goes to reach new heights with her songs is not surprising considering the attitudes her family instilled in her early on. Pious Methodists one and all, the Hills taught their kids the importance of faith. As a girl, Lauryn first began to associate singing with God when she joined her church choir and sang in gospel groups with her family.

Religion was a key component of her upbringing and provides an important clue to Lauryn's belief in herself. So long as she lived her life in a righteous way, not doing to others as she would not have done to herself, she felt happy and secure. "When I was younger I was very much in touch with God," she relayed to *Essence*. "I used to talk to Him every night."

Today, she tries to spread the Lord's word through her music. While singing in gospel choirs is a thing of her past, Lauryn is interested in much more than padding her wallet. By sharing her own experiences and mistakes with the world, she hopes to achieve her first priority: to make a difference in people's lives and turn them onto the path of redemption. That was, is, and always will be her music's ultimate goal.

Although Lauryn always felt the presence of God, there were moments in her youth that found her scared and alone. The love that surrounded her during the day, with her friends and family, dispelled the slightest possibility of fear. At night, though, Lauryn's deepest fears for herself and her family would surface. "I used to be terrified of the dark," she recalled, "and every scary thing that could possibly get you in the dark."

At such times, even her heartfelt chats with God weren't enough. After all, her family's loving company was what bolstered Lauryn's religious beliefs. Isolated in her room, she would often seek out her older brother to recapture the sense of peace and safety that she knew in the daylight hours. "I went into my brother's room and slept in the bed with him," she admitted in *Rolling Stone*. "He had football curtains and sheets. And I'd be so scared that I'd stare at those curtains and sheets and stay awake, making sure nothin' attacked us until my eyes got so heavy I had to pass out." The remnants of this intense fear would stay with Lauryn into adulthood. To this day, she can still rattle off "the colors of every single team in the NFL."

* * *

The Lauryn Hill Story

The fear of darkness and the search for enlightenment has become a recurring theme in the life and work of Lauryn Hill. While she would eventually outgrow the imagined fears that plagued her at bedtime, she has waged a lifelong battle against the all too real menace that threatens to divide her African-American brethren.

Living in South Orange, Lauryn might easily have been sheltered from the urban blight of Newark. Yet her parents would not have Malaney and Lauryn growing up ignorant of either their rich cultural legacy or the problems that faced their people. From Frederick Douglass to Malcolm X, the Hill children were steeped in the uplifting teachings of the civil rights movement's leaders. But on a daily basis, Lauryn also faced the despair and difficulties of the African-American community.

She had only to look out her attic window to see where all the tumult originated. There, in plain sight and only a short stroll away from her own grassy backyard, Newark's Ivy Hill housing project loomed large on the horizon. "I remember looking out this window," she told *Harper's Bazaar,* "and there was a certain time of day when the sun used to shine on those buildings, and they used to look like gold. Beautiful. And I'd bug, 'cause I knew they were full of wild people, kids stickin' up each other. But when something is at its worst, there's always something beautiful there too."

Sensing that hope was alive, if not always well, even in the dour projects, Lauryn would often marvel at God's mysterious ways. But she didn't rely solely on faith to prove that human kindness could coexist alongside abject poverty. She knew many of the Newark kids firsthand from playing in the public playgrounds. Paying little attention to the social position separating her from the world of public housing, Lauryn could often be found living it up among the swing sets, seesaws, and monkey bars of the projects.

Even then, she could hold her own with the big boys. Known and respected for her agility, she was a little playground legend. Her back flips inspired awe in the neighborhood children, many of whom would desperately try to match Lauryn's stunts to no avail. "I got my reputation 'cause I could flip. I was a huge tomboy," she proudly revealed to *Harper's Bazaar.*

Yet the same confidence that won Lauryn friends wherever she went also made for some perilous situations. Having grown used to being deferred to as the brightest in any given group, she was loathe to plead ignorance on any point. The phrase "I don't know" was simply not part of her vocabulary. She would eventually grow out of the know-it-all mentality, but not before learning a very important lesson.

18

Lauryn's close friend Miriam Farrakhan explained: "A bunch of us went swimming and she swore up and down she could swim. I mean, she was trying to tell *us* how to swim. So we were like 'Okay, let's see how you dive.' We threw her in and she almost drowned. Literally, almost drowned. I wanted to slap her!"

Near-death experiences aside, Lauryn's moxie has brought her the best of what life has to offer. With it, she's managed to move mountains—and who wouldn't risk life and limb for self-assurance like that? Giving credit where it's due, Lauryn never fails to attribute her strength of purpose to her family. As she told the *Illinois Entertainer,* "I think some folks have a hard time dealing with me being so young and making decisions for myself, but that's the way I was raised."

Chapter Two

The Birth of L-Boogie

Singing before a star-studded Grammy Awards audience is a long climb from wowing them at family reunions. In Lauryn's junior high days, international acclaim ranked right alongside an Ivy League education as just another dream to which she could aspire. Of course, as anyone who knows her will attest, whatever her goal, Lauryn puts all her energy into attaining it.

It wasn't enough that she had a spine-tingler of a voice. Any woman in her gospel choir could lay claim to that. No, Lauryn wanted to distinguish herself. She set out to become a songwriter. "I was in the eighth or ninth grade and I would write lyrics for instrumental pieces I heard," she recounted to the *Illinois Entertainer.* "I remember writing songs on the top of guitar solos by Carlos Santana on his album *Abraxas.* My lyrics were real mature and my mother would get on my case about them."

Valerie didn't understand where Lauryn's deep understanding of romantic turmoil came from. The girl was, after all, only a preteen at the time. Valerie's recollections of life as a twelve-year-old didn't include a sexual awakening, but times had changed. Junior high kids were experimenting with all kinds of forbidden fruit, and Lauryn's parents were worried about how the temptation would affect their daughter. "I mean with my brother my parents were like, 'Ooo, you're so fine, all the girls are gonna fight over you,'" Lauryn told *Details*. "And with me it was always, 'Girl, you better keep your legs closed!'"

Despite the double standard, Mal and Valerie had a point. With teenage pregnancy on the rise, abstinence was undoubtedly the safest way to go—for guys as well as for girls. But Lauryn's feminine imagination would find an outlet. While other girls her age stocked up on *Tiger Beat* centerfolds, Lauryn sang and wrote about love. This in itself isn't so surprising, considering that she'd been reared on heartache ever since she hit upon her mother's stash of soul music. But lamenting lost love in song was not the sole province of the old-timers. MTV and Top 40 radio offered more of the same.

When Whitney Houston rang out with "How will I know if he really loves me," millions of women, young and old alike, felt the pain. "Every little girl, including myself, wanted to *be* Whitney. I used to go out to Six Flags when karaoke was a novelty, and I must have done a hundred Whitney songs," Lauryn told *Details*. "And that sheds light, definitely, because even at nine years old I was singing songs about relationships and pain. My mother would be like, 'Girl, what the *hell* are you talking about?' "

Valerie may have been incredulous, but Lauryn knew full well what she was talking about. For not even the divine Miss Hill, awesome singer, straight-A student, and proficient back flipper all in one, was immune to schoolgirl crushes. But, heeding her mother's advice, Lauryn rarely let her heart rule her head. Instead, she vented her woes through her singing.

In time, she felt ready to take on the world. Her chance arrived in 1988. For a soul singer, there was only one place to start—Harlem's fabled Apollo Theatre. Ever since the thirties, the Apollo had provided a platform for hungry young talent. The theater's amateur contests started out as relatively informal affairs, but by the time Lauryn got her chance to shine, Amateur Night at the Apollo had become an institution. Every Wednesday, people would drop everything to give the upstarts a hard time. If the performers showed any sign of weakness, if their voices cracked, or if they lacked stage presence, the spectators would throw them to the lions. Instead of using a hook to oust the rejects from the stage, the Apollo relied on a tactic far more humiliating—the Executioner.

If the jeering persisted, the Executioner would prance onto the stage to do away with the offending performer. Only the most confident and the most foolish risked the potential mortification. But there was never any shortage of contenders at Amateur Night. Ella Fitzgerald, Gladys Knight, James Brown, Dionne Warwick, the Jackson 5—the list of celebrities who survived the Apollo's Wednesday night trial by fire goes on and on. In fact, the theater's motto is "Where stars are born, and legends are made."

Naturally, Lauryn was daunted. Adding to the pressure was the fact that the performance would be videotaped for the nationally televised program *It's Showtime at the Apollo*. In other words, millions of home viewers would be hanging on her every move and tracking her every false note. Despite her show of bravado, she was still just a thirteen-year-old girl facing a sink or swim moment. On the one hand, she knew that most of her idols had triumphed at the Apollo, and this could be her big break. On the other, she feared falling prey to the angry mob and failing miserably.

Lauryn immersed herself in a strict training regimen. First and foremost, she had to pick out her song. As an alto, she felt comfortable with the lower registers of Smokey Robinson, and decided to sing his "Who's Lovin' You" on the show. Then, for weeks prior to the big night, she exercised her voice and rehearsed her song until she had it just right. Finally, the day of the show arrived.

With knots in her stomach, Lauryn watched as her mother took complete control of the situation. In *Rolling Stone,* Valerie remembered how she "marshaled the forces, rented a big van, took a bunch of kids from her school for moral support and went off to the Apollo." Many of Lauryn's family and friends had come out to cheer her on, but she was still scared to death.

On the drive to the theater, she'd been encircled by a bevy of well-wishers, all of whom were nearly as flushed with excitement as Lauryn herself. Backstage at the Apollo, however, she was on her own. Looking out onto the stage and at the teeming auditorium was nearly enough to make her sick. Then she heard her name. This was her cue to emerge from the wings, exchange a few words with the host, sidle up to the mike, and give the performance of a lifetime. While she had the first three steps down pat, it was the fourth that presented some difficulty.

Lauryn was petrified. So much so, in fact, that she didn't even realize she was standing a good foot away from the microphone. When she overcame her fear long enough to burst into song, the audience couldn't hear a word of it. Much to her horror and absolute dismay, the crowd turned on her and began to boo. That's when she heard one voice rise above the din.

"Get close to the mike!" yelled her uncle.

According to Valerie, this was the turning point. "She grabbed the mike and sang that song with a vengeance, like 'How dare you boo me?' She sang her heart out. At the end of the song, they were clapping and screaming for her."

With the performance over, family and friends gathered around Lauryn to congratulate her, but her mood was glum. On the way back to New Jersey, she showed a brave face to her cheering section, but the sounds of the audience's booing still echoed in her ears. If only she had stood closer to the mike, the way she was taught to do, then maybe the fans wouldn't have booed, and she would have won the contest. Even though she had managed to win over the crowd, she felt like a consummate failure.

Only when the Hills arrived at their two-story home did Lauryn finally break down. Alone with her mother, Lauryn shed tears of frustration. Valerie recalled in *Rolling Stone* the words of advice she gave her daughter. "Lauryn," she'd said, "they're gonna clap for you one day . . . but you gotta take it all. This is part of the business that you say you want to be in. Now, if every time they don't scream and holler you're gonna cry, then perhaps this isn't for you."

Some advice. As if she could even think about doing anything else. The performance had not gone exactly as planned, but it had decided her life's course. Lauryn would be an entertainer, or die trying.

Lauryn's determination to perform was soon affirmed by a young man named Prakazrel "Pras" Michel. Two years her senior, he was also working hard to jump-start his own career in the music biz. While hip-hop was still playing second fiddle to pop rock in 1988, city kids such as Pras were increasingly thumbing their collective nose at the mainstream by listening to the rhythmic rhymes of Run-D.M.C., L.L. Cool J, Public Enemy, and the like. Sales of rap records had been boosted in 1986 by the Beastie Boys, who decided to sound off about the perils of suburbia on their chart-topping album *License, to Ill*. Aerosmith had also hooked up with Run-D.M.C. to record the Top 10 single "Walk This Way." For many, the popular Aerosmith ditty and the Beastie Boys' success combined to form a gateway to the more hard-core gangsta rap that was the trademark of old-school hip-hop. These urban rappers were talking about real problems—such as police brutality, drug addiction, racial conflict, and inner-city violence—and the younger generation was listening.

With the notable exception of the Beastie Boys, most of the hip-hop acts consisted of African-American MCs and DJs. At the beginning, the testosterone-powered genre that gave us break dancing, name checking, and record scratching was dominated by men. But women would soon take off with pioneers such as the wildly successful, all-female Salt-n-Pepa. By 1988, the hip-hop culture had effectively entered the fabric of daily life, and children of the sixties were aghast. The live instrumentation that baby boomers had been taught to worship seemed to have gone the way of the sit-in, and the majority were crossing their fingers in the hope that the rap-centered hip-hop experience would soon blow over.

The initial reaction to blues, jazz, and rock 'n' roll had been no different. Not surprisingly, the opposition served only to ignite the passion of hip-hop artists. With African Americans ruling the world of hip-hop, ambitious black youngsters could look to their rhyming and spinning skills for a one-way ticket out of the ghetto.

By the time Pras hit upon hip-hop, his own days in the Brooklyn projects were already a thing of the distant past. The son of Haitian immigrants who had come to America in search of refuge from their native land's totalitarian regime, Pras was a peace-loving, God-fearing denizen of South Orange with a yen for the limelight. He was in the process of forming his own hip-hop group when Lauryn was first brought to his attention. "I had this brilliant idea that two girls and one nigga would be the bomb shit," Pras later explained to *Vibe*. "Initially, it was me and this girl Marcy. We were supposed to get this girl named Tara, but I didn't like her attitude."

Luckily, Marcy was not without a backup plan. Although Lauryn was barely thirteen at the time, Marcy had heard her sing and had no qualms whatsoever about bringing her into the group. "This girl can sing," she assured Pras. "She's baaaad."

Skeptical but hopeful, Pras approached Lauryn and told her about his plans. Although soul music had always been her area of expertise, she had kept up with the rising tide of hip-hop. As a self-described "true hip-hop child," she was enticed by the opportunity to devote more time to her music. So she was only too happy to oblige Pras by coming in to sing for him. As he listened to the sound of Lauryn's voice, he could hardly believe his ears. "Out of all of the girls in our high school," Pras told the *Illinois Entertainer*, "she was the most talented. And there were a lot of talented girls at our school."

After Lauryn, Pras, and Marcy joined forces, they dubbed their group Time, and set out to find professional representation and a record deal. As no such bounty seemed to be forthcoming, the trio began to ply the New York and New Jersey nightclub circuit in their off hours. The group provided Lauryn with the perfect means of pursuing self-improvement, an opportunity to sharpen her rhymes and learn to freestyle with the best MCs in the business, but high school was an obligation that she took just as seriously. While her Time mate and fellow Columbia High School student, Pras, thought of school as "just part of life," Lauryn was hellbent on leaving a mark the size of the Grand Canyon on her school.

Teachers and guidance counselors soon noticed her drive. How could they not? Lauryn insinuated herself into every facet of Columbia High School. Using the grace given her by early dance training, she tried out for the Columbia Cougars girls' basketball team and made the starting lineup. The cheerleaders also welcomed her with open arms. She would go on to become the tri-captain of the squad. Her intellect, composure, and looks won her many admirers, and she was eventually voted class president by her peers. "Everything she touches just turns to gold," enthused her basketball coach, Joanna Wright. "We should just call her Midas."

In Lauryn's "golden child" situation, another young man or woman might easily have fallen prey to a superiority complex. But she took the popularity in stride, using her pull to help those less fortunate. She began a breakfast program for underprivileged school-age kids. The breakfast program wasn't the only thing Lauryn initiated in high school. Thanks to her efforts,

Columbia High soon boasted its own gospel choir. As always, Lauryn was the reluctant star of the show. Although she loved the sound of both her own voice and the applause it provoked, she never wanted to overshadow the efforts of others. Hence, she tried to share the spotlight as much as possible. Of course, with her sonorous voice, this wasn't always possible.

People would often single Lauryn out for her vast talent. She was even asked to sing the national anthem to kick off one of Columbia High's basketball games. After braving the stage at the Apollo, belting out a tune before her entire school was bound to be a piece of cake. The night of the game, Lauryn gave such a rousing performance that a recording of it was replayed at later games. "People went wild," recalled guidance counselor LuElle Walker-Peniston in *Time*. "I don't think we had a winning team, but *she* was inspiring."

Even as she worked to become the world's number one high school student, she managed to find time in the day for her hip-hop group. Since school and extracurricular activities kept Lauryn away from the group all day, she squeezed in her rapping practice during school hours. As her guidance counselor recalled in the Newark *Star-Ledger*, "She was phenomenal. Lauryn was a natural for hip-hop, rap talking. She loved to talk."

Articulate, opinionated, and strong, Lauryn

30

could easily have prospered as a televangelist or a motivational speaker. What she had was much more than just big talk; she had the courage of her convictions. It was this quality that earned her the respect of all who knew her. "I was not raised to be beautiful and not say it. I was not raised to have grievance and not cry out," she explained to *Vibe*. "Some people would prefer to say, 'Be pretty and don't talk too much.' But you gotta keep talking, or people forget about you and your agenda."

"Everybody knows Lauryn for her music, but they don't know about her academics," said guidance counselor Carol Bolden. Amazingly enough, Lauryn kept up a nearly perfect grade point average throughout high school, consistently ranking in the top 10 percent of her class at Columbia High School. Considering the many interests vying for her time, the scholastic success distinguished her as a true wunderkind.

Basketball, cheerleading, student government, gospel choir, her hip-hop trio, and various humanitarian efforts were not the only pursuits distracting Lauryn from her studies. By her junior year in high school, she had become a card-carrying member of the Screen Actors Guild—a triple-threat musician/actor/student. Three full-time gigs can be an ulcer-inducing experience, but the poise with which Lauryn carried out all of her responsibilities was truly a testament to her strength.

The acting began soon after her performance at the Apollo Theatre. Harking to the call of the stage, Lauryn became consumed with the idea of entertaining. Besides joining Pras's outfit, she began to scour the papers for audition notices. One day, she hit the jackpot: a casting call for *Club 12*, an off-Broadway hip-hop musical. The play was a modern interpretation of Shakespeare's *Twelfth Night* and the perfect vehicle for showcasing Lauryn's talent.

No sooner had Lauryn decided to try out for a part than she rushed to her mom with the exciting news. Never the type to hide anything of importance from her parents, she wouldn't have dared to audition on the sly. Instead of finding her own way to the casting call and dropping the bomb on her family only after the fact, Lauryn asked her parents for their blessing and their help. If she had any trepidation over revealing her intentions, they were all laid to rest. "We made a deal," Valerie recalled in the *Los Angeles Times*. "I said that as long as her schoolwork came first, I would be happy to chauffeur her to auditions and showcases."

Lauryn entered into the agreement freely and soon found herself at the off-Broadway playhouse where the auditions were being held. In keeping with the tenor of her apparently charmed life, the audition would pan out. Lauryn had her very first professional role. But luck wasn't what got her the part so much as that quality that people have since referred to as "that certain something"—in other words, talent.

Anyone who misattributed her success to a simple case of being in the right place at the right time would soon have reason to think again. While Lauryn's part in the show was by no means large, and the show itself was hardly a success, her unmistakable stage presence would attract the eye of a talent agent. With thousands of fame seekers constantly moving to New York, finding representation in the city has never been easy. Even though Manhattan boasts hundreds of agencies, actors can make the rounds until their heads are spinning and still come up empty-handed. Fortunately, Lauryn suffered no such fate. With acting ability and the rare combination of exotic beauty and wholesome girl-next-door appeal, she was every talent scout's dream.

After one night's performance, the agent made a beeline for the young performer. Inundated with promises of riches and glory, neither Lauryn nor her parents knew what to think. But since the agent was legit, and Lauryn's schoolwork did not appear to be suffering, they decided to give the casting machine a shot.

If the sixteen-year-old's life had been full before, it was nothing compared to the whirlwind into which she was thrown by her agent. Every week brought a new opportunity and a renewed sense of expectation. Finally, Lauryn's innumerable pilgrimages to New York auditions paid off. As Valerie recalled in *Entertainment Weekly,* "She went on a few auditions and some go-sees, and the next thing you know, she had a part on a soap opera."

Everything had happened so fast and come so easy that Lauryn was nearly fooled into thinking that soap opera roles were being handed out on street corners. Of course, that was far from the case. Ever since 1956, when *As the World Turns* first aired, countless hopefuls had vied for a spot on the popular program. Very few ever succeeded. Landing the recurring role of Kira Johnson was truly a cause for celebration for Lauryn, her family, and the talent agent who'd believed in her.

While most working actors must content themselves with roles in obscure plays and a commercial here and there, Lauryn had achieved the dream. It is a well-known fact that many daytime television actors go on to bigger fame. Demi Moore, Luke Perry, and Robin Wright Penn are just three examples of which Lauryn was well aware. The small screen had also given birth to quite a few successful musical artists. In short, there was no end to the possibilities presented by this key stepping stone. All Lauryn had to do was reach for them.

Becoming a fully employed actress meant great changes for Lauryn. To keep up with the daytime drama's shooting schedule, she could no longer attend classes from eight o'clock in the morning until three o'clock in the afternoon, as was required of most students. Fortunately, Columbia High School's administration understood her plight and made every allowance so she could wrap up her school day by noon.

All of her junior year was spent going to school in the morning and then shuttling to and from Manhattan. Her evenings, however, were dedicated to her first love—performing with the hip-hop group that had by now become near and dear to her heart. In three years' time, the trio she had formed with Pras and Marcy had undergone some substantial changes. Instead of two girls and a guy, the group now consisted of Lauryn, Pras, and a newcomer: Pras's cousin Nelust Wyclef "Clef" Jean.

Even the name had changed. No longer called Time, the group picked the far edgier Tranzlator Crew as their moniker. The catalyst of change was none other than Pras's talented cousin. At twenty-one years of age, Wyclef was a full five years older than Lauryn and three years older than Pras. The seniority was evident in his advanced musical acumen. He was an adept composer, a master of six instruments, and rhymed like a natural-born poet.

Much like his cousin, Wyclef had spent most of his teenage years shooting for the stars. But unlike Pras, who grew up in the States, his boyhood had unfolded amid the rancorous squalor of Port-au-Prince, Haiti. Until the age of eight, his musical education consisted of makeshift instruments that he built from found objects such as bottles and pipes. When the seven members of the Jean family first set foot on U.S. soil as illegal immigrants, Wyclef spoke nary a word of English. Haitian Creole, a French dialect, was his native tongue. The language barrier was the first of many obstacles that he'd have to overcome on his way from the illegal alien stronghold of Miami to the gang-infested housing projects of Coney Island, Brooklyn.

In time, Wyclef's father got green cards for himself and his kindred, and transported the family to Newark. He also sought out the company of his relatives, the Michels, and Wyclef and his cousin Pras were often thrown together at church and family functions. The two bonded and shared dreams.

When Pras began his freshman year in high school, it wasn't at Columbia—where he'd later make the acquaintance of Lauryn—but at Newark's Vailsburg High, where Wyclef was already a student. By virtue of their mutual involvement in the swing choir, the two soon grew closer and even spoke about merging their talents in a hip-hop group. At that point, though, it was all just talk. Vailsburg High soon closed down for lack of funding. Pras went on to earn his high school diploma at Columbia, while his cousin, much to the consternation of his devout father, a minister, continued to pursue his musical endeavors.

One fateful day, in 1991, Pras invited his cousin to come to the studio where Time laid their tracks. Having come up short with their last demo tape, the group was still trying to put together a solid showcase for their act. As Pras recalled in *Vibe,* "He came to the studio and dropped his vocals on one of our tracks. The producer we were working with at the time was, like, 'Y'all need to be a group.' We said . . . 'I'd rather deal with my own family anyway.' "

By the time Lauryn met up with Wyclef, she was an accomplished woman by any standard. It's difficult to imagine how this paragon of perfection who balanced her acting, singing, and academic careers with effortless ease could have ever felt insecure. Yet, insecurity was what pushed Lauryn all her life. She needed to be the best, to seek out challenges, and to prove to herself that she had what it took to triumph. The older and musically wiser Wyclef presented that challenge.

Having won some distinction for his song-writing in high school and being a veteran of a few rather progressive rap groups, Wyclef could play guitar beautifully and surpassed even Lauryn as an MC. True to form, she couldn't take second place lying down. From the beginning of Clef's induction into the group, Lauryn set her mind to matching her new friend's rhyming skills word for word, and a friendly spirit of one-upmanship filled the studio. For his part, Clef was duly awed by Lauryn's vocal stylings. "When I heard Lauryn sing," he told *Essence,* "I was like 'Wow!' It clicked. I knew it was meant to be."

The threesome was a true family affair. Lauryn was nothing less than a sister to the two cousins, referring to herself as "Haitian by association." Thus any competition within the group had more in common with sibling rivalry than it did with the usual conflict featured on a VH-1 *Behind the Music* installment. Soon, Pras and Clef weren't the only ones with nicknames: Anointed "L-Boogie" ("L" for short) by her Tranzlator Crew consorts, Lauryn's last rite of passage was complete. She was an official member of the hip-hop music scene.

Chapter Three

Amazing Grace

If truth is indeed stranger than fiction, then no one exemplifies the maxim better than Lauryn Hill. Any screenwriter trying to spin a yarn of a young woman leading three lives—one as a singer/songwriter, another as a television actress, and yet a third as a straight-A high school student—might well be laughed out of the room. Lauryn, however, was no ordinary girl.

Perhaps it was her strong connection to God that enabled her to rise above the rabble, or it may have been her stable family life that allowed her to sink all her energy into her careers. Whatever the secret to her success, there is little doubt that her track record was flawless. Mere mortals were agog over her superhuman concentration.

Despite her impressive activity roster, Lauryn wasn't always the consummate "Miss Thang" that she is today. Sure, she outdistanced most kids her age in the talent and dedication departments, but when it came to running her personal life, she was as confused as the next young woman. In high school, looks and boys were important—no two ways about it. In *Details*, Lauryn described her fourteen-year-old mentality: "I thought that if a guy didn't whistle at me, that meant I wasn't pretty."

In the grand tradition of James Dean, Marlon Brando, and even early John Travolta, bad boys were the ones to make her high school heart skip a beat. "When I was fifteen," Lauryn recalled, "I would've said, 'Child, if he doesn't make you swoon and explode in the air with bright lights, then you're just wasting your time.' "

Although Lauryn would discover the error of her ways sooner than most, the hormonal frenzy of adolescence obviously hit her head-on. One would think that with her busy schedule, there was no way she could pencil in time for dating. Yet, even as she juggled her various responsibilities without skipping a beat, she was also in the throes of a sexual awakening, complete with her first serious boyfriend. While she didn't tell her mother at the time, who would surely have flipped had she known, Lauryn didn't leave high school with her virtue intact. "I always felt very guilty about it because I was one of those girls who was like 'No no no—we *can't*.' "

The relationship, sparks and all, wore on for some months before Lauryn realized that the guy was a player. Three years older than Lauryn, this first boyfriend wasn't always honest, and despite her naïveté Lauryn suspected that he was unfaithful. Not one to suffer liars, she called a halt to the relationship. "I ended up dumping him," she said, "when I found out he wasn't about what I thought he was about—me."

Judging by the songs on her debut solo album, this would not be her last romantic disappointment. Yet despite the series of failed relationships that she decries on *The Miseducation of Lauryn Hill*, she managed to keep her head through it all. Which is not surprising, considering how much she was able to accomplish in the midst of her very first failed love affair.

With the addition of Wyclef, Pras's musical group looked like it was about to graduate from headlining at dives to the big time. Recording demo tapes by day and performing at clubs by night, Pras (by then a philosophy student at Rutgers University), Wyclef, and Lauryn were burning the candle at both ends trying to score a management deal. To make good on the bargain she'd struck with her parents, Lauryn often found herself doing homework in the most bizarre places. "I remember doing my homework in the bathroom stalls of hip-hop clubs," Lauryn recalled in *Teen People*.

Desperate times called for desperate measures,

and if doing schoolwork on the run was what it took to bring the Tranzlator Crew closer to their dream, then Lauryn was prepared to do exactly that. While having a manager to call their own wouldn't automatically guarantee a record contract, it was the first vital step toward that end. Ideally, a band manager takes care of the business side of a musical group, allowing the artists to focus on their music. For 10 percent of the gross wages, managers work themselves ragged booking gigs, coordinating publicity, and contacting record companies on behalf of their clients. If the act never gets off the ground, then all the manager's work is for naught. Since they can easily wind up losing money on labor and costs, professional band managers are incredibly careful whom they choose to represent.

Fortunately, Wyclef proved to be a virtual wellspring of creativity. His recruitment improved the group's sound and stage act as well as increased their local following. Their vitality and zest for performance were infectious. Wherever they played, crowds went wild. Sooner or later, the right people were bound to notice. As it turned out, the trio didn't have to wait long. Only months after reconfiguring themselves into the Tranzlator Crew, Lauryn and her two confreres were energizing another club audience when they were spotted by a talent scout from DAS Communications.

Guiding the careers of top-caliber musicians

such as the Spin Doctors of *Pocket Full of Kryptonite* fame, DAS was a force to be reckoned with in the music industry. David Sonenberg, the company president, had been in the business for years and had the monolithic Rolodex to prove it. After seeing the threesome perform firsthand, he clinched the deal. The Tranzlator Crew was officially on DAS Communications' roster.

Lauryn, Wyclef, and Pras were beside themselves with glee. They had been so nervous on the day of their private audition for David Sonenberg. So much had hinged on his reply. All three had been working toward this opportunity their entire lives. To have it all work out in their favor was nothing short of a dream come true.

At last, they would have a real chance to bring their music and their socially conscious message to all of America. As Lauryn said in *Interview*, "Our podium, what we have to speak from, is the music." If no one heard their music, then no one could be influenced by their words. While they loved to craft their songs in the modest comfort of the Booga Basement Studio in East Orange, New Jersey, the Tranzlator Crew was not fooled into thinking that the music was an end in itself. Enlightening the wayward masses—many of whom thought that drug dealing and gold digging were the way to salvation—was their platform. Come what may, the trio was determined to stick to it. And now that DAS Communications believed in them, they had every reason to believe that the people would, too.

Unbeknownst to the group, one of their fans was already working behind the scenes to get them a record deal. Her name was Rose Mann, and she worked in the retail marketing division of a small Philadelphia-based start-up label called Ruffhouse Records. She had a Tranzlator Crew demo tape, and meant to get them a hearing with the higher-ups, CEO Chris Swartz and President Joe Nicolo. In an interview with CNN, Swartz thought back to 1992 and recalled that Mann "was very passionate about this tape, and she said, 'You have to check this act out.' "

After giving the Tranzlator Crew a listen, Ruffhouse didn't waste any time getting down to business. Within days, they had contacted DAS Communications and set up an audition. When Lauryn heard the good word, she tried her best to keep calm. After all, just because a record company showed interest did not mean they were going to be given a deal. Still, the very fact that someone out there had seen her group's potential was exhilarating. And there was always the chance that Ruffhouse would decide to sign them.

Wyclef and Pras felt the same way. On the

day of their showcase, the three friends rode into town encased in a bubble of pure nervous energy—all of which they proceeded to unleash upon the unsuspecting CEO and president of Ruffhouse. "We went into the management office," Swartz told CNN, "and the group performed for us live in the office, and they were jumping around all over the place and they did this incredible live show. . . . [We] really dug them a lot, and so we decided to sign them."

It was the single greatest day of Lauryn's professional life. She'd been singing with Pras for four years now and finally had something substantial to show for it all. Nothing in her acting or academic career had ever prepared her for the happiness she would feel upon landing a record contract. More than anything else, music was her life's blood.

Although Ruffhouse was a small label, it packed a powerful commercial punch. Swartz and Nicolo had a knack for sniffing out viable talent. Having been responsible for bringing acts such as the Anglo-Latino rap group Cypress Hill and the preteen rap duo Kriss Kross into the platinum dimension, the pair had scored a production deal with the immense Columbia Records. As Swartz explained, "It's a two way thing: we deliver [Columbia Records] great, long-term, career acts, and they help provide a lot of worldwide marketing promotion that enables us to sell the little label like we need to sell—you know, fourteen million records world-wide on a given act."

So the little label wasn't so little after all. With Columbia's backing, there was no telling where the Tranzlator Crew could go.

While the future was wide open, the Crew wasn't going anywhere without a finished album. Up to now, they'd only heard tales of recording under the auspices of a record company. They had even begun to wonder whether they'd ever get the chance to experience the process. Working with a professional producer and seeing their raw material take shape under the guiding hand of a studio expert, all of it sounded so new and exciting. They couldn't wait to get started.

Work on the album began as Lauryn was entering her senior year at Columbia High School. Her role on *As the World Turns* recently had been written out, and none too soon, for she was finally ready to immerse herself fully in her music. Of course, that didn't mean that she would be letting her grades slide anytime soon. Pras managed to be in two places at once, working toward his bachelor's degree and on the album at the same time. Lauryn would do likewise: she loaded up on advanced placement courses in high school and kept her eye on college. The recording contract had not diminished her zeal for learning.

The Lauryn Hill Story

Lauryn may have been ready to bid acting a temporary adieu; however, her agent had other ideas. With a soap opera role under her belt, Lauryn was a hot commodity. Casting directors armed with Lauryn's head shot and résumé often called her agency asking for a closer look. No agent worth his business card would ever deny a client the opportunity to rub elbows with a casting director. Lauryn herself was in no position to look down her nose at high-paying assignments. She continued to go on auditions and quickly won another role.

The part was low on visibility but high on prestige. She would be playing an elevator operator in Steven Soderbergh's *King of the Hill*. Set in St. Louis during the Great Depression, the film depicted the trials and tribulations of a twelve-year-old boy who must fend for himself after being left without parental supervison. Lauryn's character was a gum-chomping elevator girl who stares into space as she talks to the young protagonist on his rides up to his landing. The whole part didn't amount to much more than three minor scenes, but the chance to work in a feature film with an acclaimed director made it well worth the effort.

Back in 1989, Soderbergh had single-handedly delivered the independent film industry from art-house oblivion with his *Sex, Lies, and Videotape*. The film had brought the Sundance Film Festival (where it won the prestigious Audience

Award) international repute and turned independent features into a cornerstone of the entertainment business. Having cost a mere pittance to produce, the movie raked in millions in ticket and video sales. After securing the Grand Prize at the Cannes Film Festival, Soderbergh and his magnum opus became the darlings of critics and audiences everywhere, and no one ever looked at small-budget, independent films quite the same way again.

Although music ruled her heart, Lauryn couldn't help getting excited over being cast in her first motion picture. Her shooting schedule would be minimal, a few days at the most, but the part would lend additional weight to her actor's résumé. A year later, the film would be released to lavish critical acclaim, but very few people would venture to see it. Not that it made much difference to Lauryn's career: Even if the movie had broken box-office records, the chances were slim of anyone remarking upon her momentary appearances on-screen.

Classes, auditions, studio work—Lauryn's life went on just as before. Of course, she wouldn't have had it any other way. Well, maybe there was one thing she would have changed if she had the chance. It had to do with, of all things, her group's new album. As she told Amazon.com, "I was very young and very naive when I came into the business and probably not as prepared as I should have been. There's a lack of scruples that you sometimes encounter in this business because there's so much money involved."

She may very well have been referring to the mishandling of production on *Blunted on Reality,* the rap trio's debut CD. The producers working with the group at the time had very definite thoughts on how the album should unfold. Unfortunately, those concepts conflicted with what Wyclef, Lauryn, and Pras stood for. The whole idea was to mold the group into what was happening at the time. The producers figured that *Blunted* would be a surefire success if they stuck to the generally accepted hard-core rap recipe, with a pinch of reggae, a splash of calypso, and a dash of dance hall thrown in for good measure.

Faced with the wisdom of their seniors, our three heroes could only look at each other and shrug their shoulders in uncertain resignation. Who were the Tranzlator Crew to argue with the professionals? What did they know about making records? For all intents and purposes, they were nobodies who knew nothing. In short, the musicians kept their opinions to themselves and did as they were told.

"You know," Lauryn told *Pulse!,* "there's a lot of pressure, particularly in R&B and rap, to produce hits. Most of us are very young, and rather than rock the boat, we do what is expected, the formulaic, because that's the easy thing to be successful [with] and that's the way to get a record deal. These days the music industry doesn't have the same patience it used to have to develop talent, so you think you've got to do what's expected."

As the days of recording turned into months, and the young artists felt their creative faculties stifled by the forces of oppression in the studio, they turned their creativity to another matter—their name. Early on, they had picked the name Tranzlator Crew to symbolize their sense of being strangers in a foreign land. Bringing Caribbean influences to bear on their music, the cousins saw the name as indicative of the group's sound. In fact, Wyclef's first hip-hop group had rapped in six languages, and considering that he had learned to speak English by listening to rap's earliest hit, the Sugar Hill Gang's 1980 ditty "Rapper's Delight," the name had seemed apropos to Lauryn as well as to her Haitian compatriots.

Now the threesome had another idea. Although the Tranzlator Crew tag had served them well, it was time to retire the moniker in favor of Fugees. The name is short for refugees, and according to Wyclef, they picked it "because when we were growing up, people used to call us refugees—as if we were the only people seeking refuge from our land. What we're saying is that everyone is a refugee, whether mentally or physically, from your country, from your life. And it's in that sense that our music is refugee music."

Other issues also played a part in the change. The new name would strike a blow against the xenophobia that had marred Wyclef's childhood. He and Pras were proud of their heritage, and incorporating it into their group's name was the ultimate proof of their patriotism. "I'm one of those patriotic Haitians who'll let you know in a minute where I'm from," explained Wyclef. The name could, of course, also be extrapolated to include all of black America's struggle to achieve the American Dream. As Pras explained to *Essence*, "As people of African descent, we are all refugees. Everyone came to this country on a boat at one time or another."

With their debut album still in production, there was no time like the present to assume the new name. All three agreed that their latest name was a winner. From that point on, they performed and recorded only as the Fugees.

While the group played on, gigging around the very joints that had given them their start, their studio work came to a standstill after the Fugees presented Ruffhouse with *Blunted on Reality*. Usually, the finished product doesn't take more than a few months to enter the marketplace. But Lauryn, Wyclef, and Pras would have to wait nearly a year for the 1994 debut of their CD.

Given the circumstances, they felt that they'd turned in their best work. All that was left to do now was wait. Always resourceful, Lauryn kept boredom at arm's length by delving into her other interests with gusto. She was in her senior year, and graduation was just around the corner. Informational brochures from universities nationwide had been finding their way into her mailbox for months, and the time to send out her college applications was now upon her.

Since she was applying for a veritable cornucopia of brand-name schools, the admissions process involved much more than filling out a simple form and making sure that she had indicated the correct GPA and standardized test scores. The time-consuming undertaking would require long essays, letters of recommendation from her teachers, and often face-to-face interviews with the admissions personnel.

While she might have known that with her academic record, extracurricular activities, and professional background, she was a shoo-in for any school, Lauryn wasn't taking any chances. Her brother, Malaney, was already bound for law school and fast on his way toward making Mal and Valerie proud. Lauryn intended to follow suit. She had been blessed with some of the greatest parents her side of the Mississippi, and she couldn't wait to give them yet another reason to smile.

At length, the thick envelopes started pouring in. One university after another was pleased to inform Lauryn that she was just the kind of mover and shaker it was looking for. Yale, Columbia, Spelman, Rutgers, the University of Pennsylvania—all were looking forward to giving Lauryn a guided campus tour.

Judging by her choice of East Coast schools, it was obvious that Lauryn had no intention of moving far away from either her family, the Fugees, or her beloved New Jersey community. But even with so many attractive options from which to choose, she had no problem making up her mind. Yale, Columbia, and the University of Pennsylvania were all Ivy League and highly selective. Spelman was an all-female, Afrocentric institution that would bring her in touch with her roots, but, while also a high-ranking school, it was located in Atlanta, Georgia. Rutgers was her New Jersey–based safety school.

Of the three Ivies, Columbia University was the closest to home. The school's prime Manhattan location was all the incentive she needed to dispatch her acceptance letter. Nothing had to change. She could still live with her parents in South Orange, sing with the Fugees in their East Orange studio, and go on auditions in New York City.

With her higher learning agenda mapped out to everyone's satisfaction, she could relax at long last. Senioritis (the condition of reduced concentration in high school seniors who have gained admission to college, a.k.a. "senior slump") was in full swing, and Lauryn was grooving to the rites of spring fever along with the rest of her classmates. Ah, to be young, beautiful, and in your last two months of high school!

If it were not for the perpetual question mark furrowing Lauryn's seventeen-year-old brow, everything would have been platinum. What would be the fate of the Fugees' album? She had not spent innumerable hours in the studio just to hear herself sing. Wyclef and Pras were also getting that antsy feeling. Just when they thought they could stand it no longer, Ruffhouse handed down the verdict. *Blunted on Reality* would be distributed in 1994, leaving Lauryn with plenty of time to pursue her educational goals before having to tour in support of the album.

With college, *King of the Hill*'s opening weekend, and the CD release party to look forward to, she could have easily put her overachieving streak on pause. But slacking off had never come easily to Lauryn, and now was no time to start. Besides, most of her endeavors were a lot more fun than they were work. Like most employed artists, she viewed her jobs as creative outlets as well as paychecks.

In this state of mind, she went on as many auditions as her talent agent could send her. She had the routine down pat. Run lines with Mom, come into the casting office, wait to be called, deliver the dialogue, go home, repeat. Because the characters were always different, acting never became dull or repetitive. She loved diving into the psyche of each new personality and trying to make her portrayal believable. Despite her small part, she had, by all accounts, done a great job in *King of the Hill*. If nothing else, that first movie proved to be a confidence-building experience. It prepared her for the bounty that was about to come her way.

The nationwide talent search for *Sister Act 2: Back in the Habit* was coming to town. The producers needed tune-carrying teens to fill the roles of inner-city parochial school students who start a thriving gospel choir. The news threw Lauryn's talent agent into a frenzy. A proven singer and an accomplished actress, Lauryn was born to star in this movie. When her agent called to inform her of the audition, she was thrilled. Not only had *Sister Act* been a hilarious romp that all America turned out to watch, but, better still, Academy Award–winner Whoopi Goldberg would come back for the sequel.

After picking up her lines at the talent agency and discussing the prospective character with her agent, Lauryn could hardly believe that she was being sent out for such a substantial role. If she won the part in the musical comedy, she'd have her own story line and ample opportunity to display both her acting and singing chops. While she would also be in for quite a payday, it was the exposure and the work itself that had her giddy with anticipation.

By the time she entered the casting office, Lauryn had the part nailed. Her reading left no doubt in the decision makers' minds: Lauryn Hill had to be in this film. When her agent called with the good tidings, the news spread like wildfire through the Hill camp. Grandparents, uncles, aunts, cousins—in short, everyone—was abuzz with talk of Lauryn's big star turn.

The first *Sister Act* had been a surprise hit. It had played in theaters all over America just one year before filming began on its sequel. In the original, brash lounge singer Deloris Van Cartier, played by Whoopi Goldberg, had audiences in stitches as she disguised herself in a nun's habit and hid out in a convent to elude the mob. In the process, she turned the convent's inept choir into a Motown-medley-belting powerhouse. No sooner had the blockbuster numbers come in than a second installment was immediately in the works. For a cool seven million dollars, Whoopi Goldberg would be coming back as Deloris, but this time she would be teaching the basics of harmony to a class of disorderly Catholic school students.

Lauryn was to play Rita Watson, the student with the heaviest chip on her shoulder and the biggest conflict. That meant that she would have her work cut out for her. Since the movie was set in San Francisco, there were also the additional drawbacks of having to work thousands of miles away from home and missing out on the last days of her senior year.

Yet, the chance to finally develop a role was too enticing to pass up. This was her first major role in a feature film, and Lauryn wasn't about to blow it. She spent months in sunny California, toiling away before the cameras. In addition to Whoopi Goldberg, her illustrious costars included James Coburn, Kathy Najimy, and the then-unknown Jennifer Love Hewitt. Surrounded by talent, Lauryn still managed to stand out on the set. Everyone from the director on down was taken with the gifted teen. "She's always been one of my favorite people—definitely one of my favorite artists," Hewitt told *Teen People*.

Lauryn's artistry was made manifest on the soundstage. In one scene, the students were supposed to rap, but Lauryn's ingenuity put the others to shame. She stole the scene, freestyling like the pro she was. Her ad-libbed rhymes stayed in the movie, and director Bill Duke had no one but Lauryn to thank for the wonderful scene. "None of that was scripted," he marveled in *Time* magazine. "That was all Lauryn. She was amazing." Whoopi herself couldn't help rhapsodizing to *Harper's Bazaar,* saying, "Lauryn is sublime."

Even when she wasn't on the set, she managed to capture the interest of entertainment industry veterans. Impressed by her positive energy and strong sense of self, costar Kathy Najimy told *USA Today* that "Lauryn was smart. At lunch, all the other kids would discuss the latest makeup or pop group; she would talk about God, really soulful." Indeed, God had never left Lauryn's side. As she would later explain in *People Magazine,* "Talking about God doesn't embarrass me. It doesn't make me less cool or less popular or corny."

She was as deeply spiritual in her teens as she'd been in her childhood. Having joined with the equally religious Pras and Wyclef, she never stood in any danger of falling in with the wrong crowd. From day one, Lauryn methodically arranged her whole life around the teachings of the Good Book, drawing upon it both for strength and for wisdom.

Chapter Four

Reality Blunts

Lauryn was primed and on the verge of fame. With a solid feature film role to her credit, the rising star could have copied many of her contemporaries and hightailed it out to Tinseltown. No doubt, other parts would have followed. Even if she never got a star on the Walk of Fame or felt the joy of having a sandwich named in her honor, she could certainly have made a good living doing something she loved. At least that's the mentality of most Hollywood up-and-comers who eschew higher education for hands-on theatrical training. But Lauryn wasn't Hollywood, she wasn't even New York for that matter; she was a Jersey girl, and proud of it.

The thought of heading west never even entered her head. Once filming of the movie wrapped, it was Columbia University that beckoned, not the City of Angels. True to her original intentions, Lauryn became a commuting student. She didn't need to live in the dorms to get the true college experience. For her, school was about learning, not drinking till the brink of dawn and squandering her valuable tuition dollars.

Since her background included Columbia High School's rigorous academic program, keeping up with her college courses wasn't difficult. Before the semester had even begun, she already knew which major to declare. Perhaps it was because she wanted so badly to make a difference in the world that she chose history as her major. Always fascinated by the subject, she sincerely believed that those who did not learn from the mistakes of the past were doomed to repeat them.

As usual, neither the acting nor the studying could keep Lauryn away from Wyclef, Pras, and their music. The three would regularly convene in their East Orange basement studio, reeling off rhymes, arranging new rap numbers, and working on their act. They were so close that Lauryn often referred to their relationship as a "three-headed child." In fact, the trio soon adopted a three-headed-baby as their group's logo.

There was no question that the Fugees were of the same mind on many subjects. The one uppermost on their collective mind was *Blunted on Reality*. More specifically, it was the album's impending release that had them on the edge of their seats. This, they thought, would be their own version of an initial public offering. Little did Lauryn know that her voice would come blasting out of CD players before *Blunted* could even reach the music critics.

When *Sister Act 2: Back in the Habit* was released in December 1993, Lauryn was in the process of prepping for her college final exams. While the sequel failed to match the grosses brought in by the original and brought a reproachful frown to the face of nearly every reviewer, Lauryn's performance received nothing but praise. With her role praised as the film's only redeeming feature, Lauryn was anything but disappointed.

How could she be when *Entertainment Weekly* opined that "the scene in which the fierce, lovely Lauryn Hill sings a few shivery bars of 'His Eye Is on the Sparrow' feels like the first genuinely religious moment in the series"? Celebrity film critic Roger Ebert was also quick to catch on, singling out Lauryn in his *Chicago Sun-Times* review for her "big, joyful musical voice and luminous smile."

That voice would find its way to the record-buying public sooner than Lauryn expected. When the movie's soundtrack was released, Lauryn was a featured player on two of the album tracks. Both "Joyful, Joyful" and "His Eye Is on the Sparrow" made generous use of her silky vocals. Back when Lauryn had been asked to perform the solos, she was too flattered by the recognition to give the consequences of her actions much thought. Certainly, she had understood that those who went to see the movie would hear her sing. But she hadn't realized that many gospel fans would buy the sound track.

She thanked God for all of it. Whenever her family, friends, and former classmates complimented Lauryn on her performances either with the Fugees or on *Sister Act 2*, she was all gracious humility. Knowing that she'd been blessed with a gift, her whole being radiated with gratitude to the higher power that had chosen her for its vessel. "I've been so successful because I respect the fact that my talent is a gift from God," she would later affirm in *Essence*. "It's cool if people give us kudos and accolades, but I know who is responsible for everything I do. All praise should be given to Him."

At last the day Lauryn and her Fugees cohorts had been waiting for had arrived. *Blunted on Reality* would be unleashed upon the unsuspecting hip-hop nation. The trio would finally have to go out on the line. Although their producers had worked some magic in the studio, the lyrics on the album were pure Fugees. Their innermost feelings and deeply held beliefs were expressed on the CD. Now it would all be offered up for general consumption.

The Lauryn Hill Story

No one knew exactly what to expect. Outside New York and New Jersey, the Fugees didn't have much of a following. Despite having played together for three-odd years, they were still a young act with minimal name recognition. Of course, many a young group has been known to explode out of nowhere by tapping into the spirit of the times. While moving a million copies of *Blunted on Reality* wasn't an altogether impossible feat, Lauryn, Pras, and Wyclef had to admit that it was not likely to happen—if only to protect themselves from disappointment.

Truth be told, even as they attempted to suppress their great expectations, all three Fugees hoped for the best. Every one of their songs was a personal manifesto. If the public failed to appreciate their candor, or worse yet, criticized and dismissed the album as irrelevant, it would be painful. To be sure, they braced themselves for this possibility. But they didn't dwell on it.

Lauryn didn't need mass approbation to believe that the Fugees were the genuine article. She had watched as the songs took shape in the studio; she knew from whence the music came. If the spirit of hip-hop was truly about keeping it real, and she believed that it was, then the Fugees' call-it-like-they-see-it style would meet with a warm welcome.

With the excitement of the CD's coming-out

party and the bad case of nerves that accompanied it, it was all Lauryn could do to focus on her term papers, textbooks, and class discussions. While she might have been a master of concentrating on the matter at hand, so much depended on the performance of the group's debut album that she had to summon all her willpower to turn her attention away from the reviews and the sales figures.

Fortunately, Lauryn had great reserves of strength from which to draw. *Blunted on Reality* was no star-making turn. The only consolation was that this fact was not evidenced by the reviews. Within the music critics' community, *Blunted on Reality* had as many proponents as detractors. In fact, even those who gave the album low marks still gave the musicians credit for potential and vision. Sadly, not many reviewers chose to put pen to paper on behalf of the album. This neglect at the hands of the mass media, coupled with the modest marketing campaign offered by the record label, ensured that hip-hop aficionados would receive little notice of the Fugees' arrival.

Although two singles would be culled from *Blunted on Reality*, "Nappy Heads" and "Vocab," neither received the radio airplay required to make it a hit. Even the accompanying videos would be largely ignored by the MTV rotation planners. Lauryn's heart sank as she watched the album enter the *Billboard* chart's nether regions. All was not lost, however, as a popular single could always help their CD rise through the ranks. It wasn't unheard of.

Alas, it was not to be. "Nappy Heads," the lead single, only climbed as far as Number 49. Consequently, the album made only a feeble impression upon the music scene, peaking at Number 62 on *Billboard*'s R&B chart. "When we did *Blunted*, in some towns we'd sell only one or two albums," Lauryn recalled in *Essence*, adding that those "were probably bought by my mother and some cousins."

All told, *Blunted on Reality* fell way below the mark, selling only a middling 130,000 copies. Lower numbers have been documented, but anything under 150,000 is purgatory in the music biz. The Fugees now found themselves in that gray area, somewhere between a recording contract and the no-man's-land of unsigned acts. Wyclef, for one, was convinced that Ruffhouse was about to show them the door. "After *Blunted on Reality*, the label was supposed to drop us," he said in the Newark *Star-Ledger*. "Somehow our live performances kept us alive. It showed them there was something more to the group than just records."

While he may have had the wrong idea about Ruffhouse, Wyclef's evaluation of the Fugees' stage show was right on the money. They were a hot act, and their fever proved highly contagious. Every joint they played was guaranteed to be jumping by the time Lauryn, Wyclef, and Pras were through with it. They were so facile with freestyle and their moves so energetic that despite *Blunted*'s poor showing, they still packed one house after another on their tour.

Lauryn loved performing live even more than recording in the studio. Although she was still a full-time student when the Fugees hit the road in support of their album, she hardly minded rearranging her schedule for the chance to represent their music. It was in the clubs that the trio really came together as a unit. Working off each other, sparks flew as they took their turns at the mike and even with instruments. All three shared the spotlight, with no sign of anyone jockeying for the lead.

Unlike in so many other hip-hop outfits, the Fugees' female member was anything but a token. Audiences were struck by the force of her delivery as an MC and embraced by the velvety richness of her song. Time and again, Lauryn's deft performance made it clear that she was not going to play window dressing to Pras's and Wyclef's displays of talent.

Their shows made consistently favorable impressions. Of course, no one can please all the people all the time. Some naysayers nitpicked at details, such as the group's choice of clothes. Most, however, enjoyed the freshness of an act that could mix so many musical styles. "This is what hip-hop needed for the music to go to the next level," Wyclef told Sony, "where you could pick up a guitar, or sing, and not feel like you've gotta front."

Wyclef hit the nail right on the head. Innovation was the group's raison d'être. Whether their first album flopped as a direct result of the production or whether, as some say, it simply caught the world unaware, the Fugees lived to see a brighter day for one simple reason—they never strayed from their original course. While working their way through the disappointment of *Blunted on Reality*, the Fugees could have resorted to any number of hip-hop clichés to make sure that they were never let down again. But gimmicks, artifice, and big bucks paled in comparison to their artistic goals. "At the time we were coming up," Wyclef later told the *Star-Ledger*, "there were a lot of kids coming out with us. None of them are around now. They didn't stick to their gut feeling and judgment."

Pushing the boundaries of rap music came with a stigma all its own. As with many experimental artists, the Fugees' talent was called into question by the champions of mainstream hip-hop. "They were calling us this 'alternative' group," Lauryn explained to *Vibe*. "And alternative, from where we come from, means no skills."

Lauryn and her Fugee compatriots felt like they had to prove their mettle in concert because some people didn't trust in their authenticity. By this time, alt-rappers such as Arrested Development and Digable Planets had used up their fifteen minutes of fame and were languishing in the bargain bins of used CD retailers. Those who'd heard of the Fugees wondered whether this band was in for the same fate.

All in all, helming the vanguard was turning out to be a thankless task. The group had not intentionally set out to lead the way. All they'd wanted was to forge their own original sound. Inexperienced in the ways of the music world, they couldn't have known that this fact alone would suffice to land them at hip-hop's outermost periphery. Pras, Lauryn, and Wyclef caught a lot of flak for sounding like self-proclaimed saviors of hip-hop's soul.

Inspired as she was by the selfless lives of Jesus Christ and Nina Simone, Lauryn remained adamant. As she explained in *Details*, "Both taught me that your thanks is not necessarily on earth, that it's a rough path to tread. I mean, Nina Simone was a revolutionary who spoke on behalf of people who probably didn't even appreciate her, and it made for a very hard, almost bitter life. And Jesus Christ? Thankless job, too—you save the world but must be crucified."

Despite their positive outlook, the Fugees were hurt to learn that no good deed goes unpunished. Of course, they still had each other. Moreover, they still had a record contract. Ruffhouse, they were relieved to learn, never doubted them for a moment. The label's continued encouragement played a key role in the group's artistic development. Here, after all, was a label that knew what they were talking about, and it was saying that the Fugees were on the right track.

Many a record company would have taken a different approach and sent the group packing. When they'd signed on to Ruffhouse, Lauryn, Pras, and Wyclef had no idea about the label's philosophy on burgeoning acts. For all they knew, their first album might well have been their last. When *Blunted on Reality* failed to ascend the charts, the Fugees held their breath, wondering if it would indeed be their only Ruffhouse release.

Lucky for them, Ruffhouse was not about to give up so soon. The fact that *Blunted* stiffed came as no surprise to CEO Chris Swartz, who knew all along that the album was but a sign of bigger things to come. "*Blunted on Reality* never had that good a chance because it was so eclectic," he told the Newark *Star-Ledger*. "The band was better than the record. We knew it wasn't as good as the live act we signed."

Once they were secure in the faith of their investors, the Fugees were free to roll with the punches. If Swartz didn't mind the modest sales, they sure as hell didn't care. Pras voiced the prevailing sentiments when he told the *St. Louis Post-Dispatch* that *"Blunted on Reality* served its purpose, whether or not you want to believe it. We're not mad at the fact that it didn't blow up. That's not what we are looking for. We're looking at longevity."

With Lauryn's record of success, the trio might have known that they were in for a break. Their change in fortune was heralded by the unexpected popularity of Salaam Remi's "Nappy Heads" and "Vocab" club remixes. Months after the release of *Blunted on Reality*, the dance floors were teeming with kids grooving to the Fugees' beat. Suddenly, radio stations were getting in on the action. Even MTV was plugging the videos.

To commercialize on this newfound success, the Fugees' management, DAS Communications, kicked into high gear, contacting club promoters and booking more gigs as well as coordinating additional publicity events. The company's biggest coup came when they scored their clients a slot as guest hosts of *Yo! MTV Raps*. For a fledgling outfit such as the Fugees, this was the mother of all opportunities.

Lauryn was only too aware of the implications of a national television appearance. Millions would see their faces, hear their words, and, hopefully, remember their name. Although the chance of this exposure translating into a platinum album was scarce, it just might pave the way for their next CD. Each member of the group was happy to sit on the MTV couch and speak into the camera. Of course, no one would have known it by looking at them. Once the cameras were rolling, the little-known trio came off as cool as bona fide rap superstars.

Flanked by Wyclef and Pras and wearing the baggiest in hip-hop couture, Lauryn looked not a day older than her nineteen years. But despite this street urchin–esque appearance, her laid-back pose spoke volumes about her place in the group. Obviously, this girl was not one of those glorified rap posse groupies. She was one of the guys.

Perhaps she was even more than that. Support for Lauryn's solo career had begun to build months before. But that paled in comparison to what followed Remi's remixes of the *Blunted* singles. In these latter versions of "Nappy Heads" and "Vocab," Lauryn's voice was highlighted to its greatest advantage. Careful listeners were blown away by the revelation. When the videos hit MTV, viewers found that putting a face to the voice only served to magnify their listening pleasure.

Since the Fugees' prospects seemed none too bright to the world at large, people began talking of L-Boogie's desertion as a done deal.

Most fans just wanted to see more of Lauryn, and they hated to see her talent squandered on a failed group. While their hearts were in the right place, Lauryn was not amused. "It's not a compliment when people tell me to break off from them," she told *Vibe*. "That's like telling me to drop my brothers. I consider these guys family, so if I act rudely when somebody suggests I go solo, don't think I'm a bitch."

What many viewed as overreaction on Lauryn's part was just her way of defending her livelihood. Suggestions that she could be a more viable artist on her own did much more than threaten her family ties; they disrupted her peace of mind. Unlike many group members who go out of their way to attract the lion's share of attention, only to deny playing any part in the media circus later on, Lauryn had never done anything to put herself before her partners. Not that she ever had to; her voice did the showboating for her.

Inevitably, Wyclef and Pras soon became disturbed by all the attention lavished upon Lauryn. Even as they took their act overseas during the summer of 1994, the Fugees were never far removed from the hurtful insinuations of the media. Whatever article they read, everyone seemed to be saying the same thing: Lauryn did not need the Fugees. "The whole industry was saying that," Pras told *Vibe*. "The critics, the people who write the magazines."

Although Lauryn made no sign of leaving and went so far as to express great dissatisfaction with the journalists who encouraged her to do otherwise, Pras and Wyclef couldn't help feeling somewhat insecure. The guys knew that they were talented, but without Lauryn the group just wouldn't be the same. She was an invaluable part of their sound, and losing her would be nothing short of disastrous. "Our music is a fusion of three styles," Wyclef explained. "L brings the soul. I bring my guitar, my awareness, my church background. And Pras brings his background."

The insult implied by the support for Lauryn's solo career ruffled the cousins' feathers. Exactly whose lyrics did people think she was singing? It wasn't all Lauryn's handiwork. Certainly, Wyclef and Pras had had a lot to do with the singles and the album. "There are always those who will try and divide a situation, but this isn't a group that was put together. We've known each other a long time," Pras told *Vibe*.

If Wyclef and Pras suspected that Lauryn was capable of bowing to external pressure, they were very much mistaken. She loved her group mates like brothers. Perhaps more important, she loved the music that the three of them made together. Back then, the very essence of her being was emotionally, spiritually, and irrevocably bound to the Fugees.

A lesser group might have deteriorated under the weight of popular opinion, but Lauryn, Wyclef, and Pras were strong. It had been nearly six years since Lauryn made her commitment to the group, and when the guys saw that she wasn't about to fold, they didn't waste any more time indulging irrational fears. The Fugees was a team effort, and they were going to move forward as such. "We didn't let the flopness of that first album break us up," Pras told the *St. Louis Post-Dispatch*. "Lauryn could have easily been like, 'I'm going solo because I can do this by myself.' But it's a family. Lauryn didn't let none of that get to her."

Aside from denying all rumors of a split, the Fugees could do nothing to either quell the industry buzz or change the direction of its current. At first, the sense of powerlessness was frustrating, to be sure. But with time, the group learned to hold the music media at arm's length. As Wyclef told *Vibe*, "If we took the stuff the critics say seriously, I would have gone back to Haiti."

There was, perhaps, one way to combat the gossip mongers. Since actions speak louder than words of denial, the Fugees' fealty could only be confirmed by a return to the studio. And that's exactly what they decided to do. "We were like 'Yo man, spiritually we're strong. Let's just go back and give our best shot on this album,' " Pras recalled in the *St. Louis Post-Dispatch*.

Giving it their best shot would mean making some major changes. By now, the trio had spent more than a year in the heart of the music industry. They were no longer the same wide-eyed innocents who'd signed the contract with Ruffhouse. What they may have lacked in commercial success, they more than made up for in experience and confidence. While recording *Blunted on Reality*, they had followed the preordained rules to no avail. Yet for all their trouble, the group did learn a very important lesson. If they were ever going to become contenders in the rap race, they would have to learn to trust their instincts.

To this end, the group agreed to cut their next album at Booga Basement Studio. Aptly enough, the studio was truly located in the basement of an East Orange house. These digs did not look like much, but Booga Basement was the Fugees' birthplace. Here, the group was always at ease and inspiration was never hard to come by.

What's more, they were going to produce the CD themselves. They had put their trust in other producers before, and it had backfired. They weren't taking that chance again. Tired of following orders, Lauryn, Wyclef, and Pras were ready to take absolute control over their product. "The production on our last album was wack," Wyclef told *Vibe*. "But for the next album, we're not working with the same people. Our next album is gonna be the bomb."

Talented and self-assured, the Fugees had all the makings of the next big thing. During the past year, the threesome had gone through the wringer. They'd recorded and released an album, then stood helplessly by as that album fizzled on the charts and the longevity of the group was brought into question. They'd also met many of hip-hop's megastars, lived a bit of the glamorous life, and seen the seamier side of fame up close and personal. From these experiences, they had extracted not a few important truths. They were older, they were wiser, and they were about to put their newfound knowledge to use.

Going into her sophomore album with the Fugees, Lauryn knew that the group already had one strike against them. Pras and Wyclef were also fully briefed on the dire state of their communal affairs. Their future in music was now at stake, and it was time to do or die. Had they been without a plan, the group might have panicked. As things stood, however, the trio was as calm as three crickets on a summer's eve.

Taking matters into their own hands was all the strategy they needed. All three were convinced that, given free rein, they could ante up a CD that the world would not soon forget. Whereas *Blunted on Reality* had been criticized for its lack of focus, the Fugees knew that their next effort was going to be different. Why? Because they themselves were different.

The group had, over time, developed into one of the most professional and sophisticated ensembles in all of hip-hop. Onstage, the MCs' impulses were invariably in sync. They had

77

even found a way to make the merging of their disparate sonic styles appear effortless. Couched in these auditory refinements, the Fugees' message, which had not changed one iota, would pack a powerful punch.

As their first self-governing act, the group assembled their backup crew by calling on musical friends and relatives, such as Wyclef's bass-playing cousin Jerry Duplessis. Their next order of business was to plan the actual content of the album. Several informal gatherings at Booga Basement gave rise to the million-dollar-idea that had Lauryn waxing rhapsodic. She described the concept to Sony as "an audio film. It's like how radio was back in the Forties. . . . It tells a story, and there are cuts and breaks in the music. It's almost like a hip-hop version of *Tommy*, like what the Who did for rock & roll."

The goal was certainly a lofty one. Considering the progressive nature of the Who's rock opera *Tommy*, Lauryn's words made it clear that the Fugees would continue trying to push hip-hop forward. No longer abashed by the superficial labels with which the public chose to classify them, they blocked out the irrelevant outside interference and concentrated on the sound. "If you want to call us 'alternative,' so be it," Lauryn told *Vibe*. "We're trying to bring musicality back to the 'hood."

In order to strike the perfect chord with their next album, Lauryn, Wyclef, and Pras traveled back in time. They studied a variety of musical genres and borrowed ideas from the music of yesteryear. Their mission was to build upon the past.

As Wyclef explained to the Newark *Star-Ledger*, respect was due to all the music under the sun. "Basically," he said, "you need a good sound whether it's hip-hop, rap or R&B. Rappers talk negative about R&B records, [but] they wouldn't have anything to sample from without R&B. You have to know the history and understand."

With their firm grasp of music past and present, the group was ready to collaborate and create. But before Lauryn could begin, she would have to tie up some loose ends.

Once the "Nappy Heads" and "Vocab" remixes caught the public's attention, the Fugees were suddenly in demand. Club promoters became more receptive and the group's itinerary more action packed. With an eye on recording a follow-up album, Lauryn felt that her time at Columbia was coming to an end.

Her first year at the school had been a whirlwind of activity. First semester, she'd hit the books while completing *Blunted on Reality*. Second semester, she'd juggled her schoolwork with the demands of touring. Then, the remixed versions had burst upon the scene, and the

Fugees ascended to the next level of stardom—minor celebrity. The influx of work was immediate, and Lauryn began to entertain second thoughts about her collegiate plans.

She understood the value of education. Most of her family had attended college, and furthermore, her mother was a teacher. But to stubbornly pursue her bachelor's degree at this point and time could well prove to be an exercise in futility. Even if she managed to maintain her grades with intense cram sessions, she couldn't possibly appreciate or retain the information if her heart and mind were elsewhere. With the recording of the Fugees' second album drawing nigh, Lauryn realized the impossibility of the task before her.

The lives of recording artists move at the speed of sound; as soon as their music reaches an audience, they are expected to show up in person. The schedule of a full-time college student, especially an Ivy League college student, is no less hectic. It's an avalanche of quizzes, tests, reading material, and research papers. Both lifestyles require the participant's complete attention. Normally, the twain never meet.

While Lauryn had managed to combine the world of higher learning with her musical aspirations for one whole year, she was left frazzled and burnt out. Now that her career was really taking off and she was planning to coproduce her first album, there was absolutely no way to sustain her double life. It all boiled down to one choice: Columbia University or Columbia Records?

What would have been a no-brainer for many up-and-comers proved to be a real brainteaser for Lauryn. After all, her serious approach to academia was the whole reason for the dilemma. If she'd been content to just coast by with a C average and have nothing but a degree to show for her efforts, she may have decided to remain in school while working with the Fugees. But she had genuine respect for learning. As she said on Fugees.net, "Education is a means to free your mind and not have to depend on anybody else."

She grappled with the decision for some days before making it public. Since Columbia University wouldn't shed any tears over the loss of one undergraduate, whereas the Fugees certainly would, Lauryn's loyalties belonged with her brothers, Wyclef and Pras. She figured that once things slowed down, school would still be there.

Naturally, Mal and Valerie had some doubts. Coming back to school after a prolonged leave of absence can be difficult. But they understood. In fact, they'd been expecting something like this for months. Watching their daughter rushing off to school every morning, only to sequester herself in the studio with the Fugees every other night, was almost as hard on them as it was on Lauryn. If she didn't think that she could carry on at this pace, then no one in the Hill household was going to push her.

In truth, Lauryn never really had a choice, and college never really stood a chance. To drop the Fugees would have been to sever her main creative artery. After years of jamming with the guys, she couldn't imagine life without them. So she said good-bye to Columbia and devoted her life to the group.

As work on the new album got under way, Lauryn's role within the Fugees was expanded. On *Blunted on Reality*, her contribution had been somewhat limited. While Pras and Wyclef had collaborated on nearly every track of that CD, Lauryn's part involved more singing and rapping than anything else. All that was about to change.

Now that she no longer had to divide her attention between school and music, she was eager to try her hand at production. She would also be bringing her fair share of rhymes to the table. While no one had any doubt that L-Boogie was much more than the Fugees' lawn ornament, she still felt that her gender often relegated her to the back of the proverbial bus. "Look," Lauryn told *Pulse!*, "there's sexism in the world and the music industry is just a microcosm of that. Men don't necessarily count on you to think in this business."

Although Pras and Wyclef treated her as an equal, many in the music business often assumed that Lauryn's talent was limited to her vocal cords. "It's as though men can write 'serious compositions' but women just sing 'cute little ditties,' " she complained to *Showbiz*. By putting her stamp on the Fugees' product and showcasing the full extent of her repertoire, she hoped to combat such misogynic misconceptions. More important, she rightly believed that she had a lot to offer in terms of both vision and skill.

Lauryn's years with the Fugees had turned out to be time well spent. When she first began her tenure with the group, it was her voice that Pras was after. Back then, she didn't know the first thing about being an MC. "Rhyming . . . that's something actually I developed when I met Clef and Pras," she said on Fugees.net. "I sang first, but the rapping is really important to me." Now, Lauryn could rock the house with the best of the b-boy wonders, and she didn't intend to hold back.

The songwriting aspect of recording wasn't as new to Lauryn as the producing and arranging. As she tried her hand at manning the control boards, she couldn't help feeling like a pioneer, as if she were going where no woman had gone before. Since female record producers are truly a rarity in the industry, Lauryn's feelings were not unjustified. In word and in deed, she was taking a giant step for womankind.

Nonetheless, the effects of her actions would not be felt for some time. As long as Lauryn was surrounded by men, there would be people who'd persist in giving all the credit to her Y-chromosomed partners. But she didn't worry about any of that while working with Pras and Wyclef. They knew her contribution was solid. That's all that really mattered.

Satisfied as she was with the attitude of her own crew, Lauryn still struggled to edify the world at large on the importance of feminist issues. The hip-hop community is especially prone to denigrating the fairer sex as "bitches" and "hos." This, Lauryn felt, was at the root of her race's problems. If men disrespect women, then the relationship most fundamental to the progress of civilization is inherently flawed. "It's not as though strong female role models aren't out there, be it Scary Spice or whatever," she told *Showbiz*. "The problem lies in the way that people speak about women."

Sure enough, Lauryn wasn't the only woman MC in the business. To highlight the female factor, she agreed to participate on Big Kap's album *Ladies in the House*. At the time, Bahamadia and PreCise were already taking part in the project, and Lauryn was eager to join in the all-female review. Many mistook this independent action for a restless stirring, and the Fugees were again placed on twenty-four-hour separation watch.

For Pras and Wyclef, the constant emphasis on Lauryn was a bitter pill to swallow. Since the threesome spent most of their waking hours together, conflict was bound to rear its ugly head. No doubt, more than a few of the group's arguments found their root in Lauryn's preeminence in the media. "I was young and naive, and it caused some stress within the group," Lauryn later told *Vibe*. "I felt that because I paid no attention to it, that meant other people didn't pay attention to it. Who knows what insecurities are in the minds of people because of what someone says? In my mind, I was happy because those were my boys; we grew up together. I loved them very much. But, you know, the hill looks different depending on where you're standing—if you're at the bottom or at the top or in the middle."

Other disagreements were a simple by-product of three distinct personalities working as one unit. "In any group you're going to have different dynamics, throughout the history of their group," Lauryn explained to *Horizon Magazine*. "We have real relationships and when you have real relationships, as opposed to relationships that are put together and forced together, you're always going to have issues."

But even as they struggled to come to terms

with their individual issues, the Fugees never ceased to care about one another. In *Vibe*, Pras recalled the day that they recorded "Ready or Not," saying that "the three of us was each going through some pain. L was crying when she did her vocals. It was unbelievable. To see her singing with tears coming out of her eyes, it made me want to cry too."

This was not one of those ensemble acts whose members seem to relish hanging their dirty laundry out to dry. Their problems were nobody's business but their own. So, no matter what their differences, the group presented a unified front to the public. Years later, as evidenced by her interview with the *Washington Times*, Lauryn would still be saying, "Nah, don't expect me to complain about the Fugees."

As days turned into months and the album took shape, Lauryn was amazed at what the group had been able to accomplish. Even to her critical ear, the tracks sounded pristine. It was then that the Fugees decided to leave more than good enough alone. In November 1995, they turned their masterpiece over to Ruffhouse.

When Lauryn, Pras, and Wyclef assembled to face the press in a Columbia Records conference room, Wyclef was confidence personified. While Lauryn and Pras would only venture to guess that the sales of their new album would exceed those of *Blunted on Reality*, their fellow Fugee had bigger visions. "The mass of people, that's what's going to make the Fugees," he told *Vibe*. "And that mass you can't stop, because the music we're doing, we doing it for them. Somewhere on this planet, this album will win."

This sense of certainty was, perhaps, what led the group to name their second effort *The Score*. Fortunately, the fates would decide to smile at their show of bravado, and the title would prove prophetic. At the time, however, they couldn't have known exactly how impressive a score the record would be. Since the CD was not slated for release until February 1996, the Fugees would have to sweat out the suspense for another three months.

Despite the importance of surpassing *Blunted on Reality*, the group mates didn't lose much sleep over the final outcome. Although they would have liked their album to be well received, they knew that *The Score* was their very best work to date, that they hadn't compromised their artistic integrity to make it, and that it expressed everything they'd wanted it to. Never mind the sales figures, to Lauryn, Wyclef, Pras, and everyone who'd lent a hand in the studio, the album was already a smashing success.

They had agreed that their first single would be "Fu-Gee-La." The stirring cut mixed Lauryn's vocals and the Fugees' trademark verbal harangues within an ambience of futuristic instrumentation. It was just the thing to make people take notice.

No sooner had the lead single hit the radio than the rave reviews began pouring in. *Entertainment Weekly* gave *The Score* an "A," calling it a showcase of the group's "acrobatic lyrical technique and restless intelligence." On a scale of one to ten, *Spin* rated the album a nine, saying that a "sense of organic interaction is the hallmark of this album." *Q Magazine* pitched in their two cents by calling the CD "an impressively panoramic soundscape, mixed into a thirteen-track seamless whole." Even the normally conservative *Time* magazine stated that the Fugees "cross cultural and musical boundaries to create a sound that is bold and fresh."

When *The Score* was finally released on February 13, 1996, the single and the positive press notices sent 71,000 record buyers scurrying to the stores, ready to lay down their cash for the Fugees. Not too shabby for one week's release. Since Lauryn, Wyclef, and Pras shared the lead production and songwriting credits on the album, such sales stats could have translated into a tremendous windfall for the group. But instead of greedily rubbing their palms and counting their soon-to-be-hatched chickens, the trio focused on bringing the music to the fans.

For Lauryn, the favorable response was a relief of unmatched proportions. For some time,

Fugees at All Star Cafe

Muhammad Ali at *When We Were Kings* premiere

In Haiti, 1997 benefit

With Stevie Wonder at
39th Annual Grammys

Voelker/Shooting Star

Agostini/Gamma Liaison

Moskowitz/Globe

Paniccioli/Retna

Paniccioli/Retna

Five Grammys, February 1999

Grammy for Best New Artist 1999

Presenting the 1999 R&B Foundation Award to Patti LaBelle

Accepting the 1999 Soul Train Music Award for *The Miseducation of Lauryn Hill*

With Rohan Marley at Jingle Ball, December 1998,
New York City

her years of hard work—her entire musical career—had hung in the balance. At last, her prayers had been answered. But Lauryn's brightened spirits did not have as much to do with the fame and wealth portended by *The Score* as with the long-awaited guarantee of a future in the record industry. The upsurge in popularity meant that the Fugees would no longer have to struggle just to keep their heads above water. The group was now officially on the map, and they intended to stay there.

Spreading the Fugee gospel from coast to coast promised to be a grueling experience. The trio's management team had been booking gigs for weeks, and an extensive tour of North America and Europe was scheduled to kick off in early March. Then, after an unconscionably short break, the group was locked into the two-month Smokin' Grooves tour, which would last until September. Lauryn was tired just thinking about it.

On the various legs of their tour, the Fugees would be sharing the bill with acts as illustrious as the Roots, the Goodie MoB, and Bahamadia. Although they were playing at relatively small, 1,000-seat venues, headlining for such hot hip-hop artists was a definite sign of their growing clout. Even though "Fu-Gee-La" had not climbed higher than Number 29 on Billboard's Hot 100, the single dominated urban radio and would soon turn gold. As for *The Score*, it, too, was fast on its way to success.

At first, Lauryn was justifiably energized by the flurry of exciting news and activity that follows in the wake of a hit record. Photo shoots, interviews, sold-out shows, screaming fans— for a while there, she felt as if she were truly living the dream. The euphoria, however, would not last long. "I think for a hot minute this was exciting to me and my family," she told *Harper's Bazaar*. "But all of us are pretty much uninspired by money and material things."

God, family, love, and music had always been the cornerstones of Lauryn's existence. Although her family and her music were doing just fine, her love life as well as her bond with God were in a state of disrepair. The dysfunction in her life was rooted in romantic turmoil. She was involved in a relationship that was going nowhere fast, but she couldn't seem to break free. While Lauryn has steadfastly refused to name the man responsible for her heartache, she did tell the *Illinois Entertainer* that "no matter how much I pushed and how perfect I thought we were, [reciprocity] was the thing that was missing."

No amount of money could change that sad fact. Neither could her newfound celebrity make up for the hollow feeling in her soul. One night, after a show at L.A.'s House of Blues with he Fugees, Lauryn unburdened herself to a reporter from *Essence*. She told the journalist that she'd committed "one of the biggest sins you can do when you have such a tight relationship with God—I put someone before Him. I fell deeply in love and put a man before God."

Lauryn's triumph was bittersweet. While she had, indeed, arrived, there were many times when she couldn't so much as muster a smile. By virtue of her personal problems, she quickly learned that success and happiness don't always go hand in hand.

For Lauryn, true contentment would be long in coming. In the meantime, commercial success would have to do. During the spring of 1996, while on the European leg of their world tour, the Fugees released their second single. All of a sudden, *The Score* went flying off the record-store shelves. The group's version of Roberta Flack's 1973 hit, "Killing Me Softly with His Song," propelled Lauryn and her consorts into the ionosphere of pop superstardom.

It didn't matter whether you were white, black, Asian, Hispanic, American, or British, chances are you knew someone who purchased a copy of *The Score*. By the time Lauryn's ethereal rendering of "Killing Me Softly with His Song" had been played out, 17 million people worldwide had added the Fugees' second CD to their collection. The song was a perpetual presence on both the radio and the all-important MTV network.

The video was in heavy rotation for months on end. You couldn't so much as turn on MTV without witnessing the image of Lauryn, Wyclef, and Pras playfully pelting each other with popcorn at a movie theater. People simply couldn't get enough of Lauryn's soul-stirring siren song. They may not have known her name, but at their nightclubs and at their parties, in their cars and in their showers, people of every color and creed were listening to and singing along with that beautiful girl from the Fugees.

Again, Lauryn was the one at the center of the media blitz. The music video turned her into an instant celebrity. As the group toured the States to promote their fast-selling album, Pras and Wyclef had to endure playing second fiddle to their leading lady as she was mobbed on all sides by adoring fans. As usual, the autograph hounds only had eyes for Lauryn.

Neither was all the flattery directed at Lauryn's sizzling vocal delivery. As a famous persona, her personality was also up for vigorous discussion. Fortunately, everyone from the Fugees' roadies to established superstars had words of praise for the sincere Ms. Hill. In *Vibe*, the trio's assistant road manager described her as "the perfect black woman. . . . She has knowledge, heart, and she definitely wears her intentions on her sleeve. She lets you know where she's coming from." Hollywood icon Warren Beatty was also a believer. After one Fugees gig, he made his way backstage for the express purpose of meeting the singing sensation. The introduction impelled him to tell *Entertainment Weekly* that "she's an old soul with uncommon humility, beauty, and musicality. She's totally devoid of bullsh--."

With the whole world falling at her designer-shod feet, Lauryn could have used her limited time off to wallow in the lap of luxury and spend some of her hard-earned cash. Instead, what she did was prove that her many enamored devotees were great judges of character. No sooner had the money and star power begun to flow her way than she began thinking up ways to help her less fortunate brethren.

Clearly, fame hadn't changed Lauryn at all. She was still the noble spirit who'd used her popularity to launch a free-breakfast program in high school. Except now she could flex her music-industry muscle to work on a global scale. She did exactly that by devoting herself to the Refugee Project.

To Lauryn, the Fugee tag was much more than a cool-sounding brand name—it was a way of life. As a symbol of refugees everywhere, she felt that the group represented "the have-nots, the outsiders." She couldn't help but recognize the responsibility that came with her newfound power. Here was her chance to change the world and back up the agendas she'd propounded on the Fugees' albums.

The Refugee Project is a nonprofit organization that "encourages a change in the attitudes and social agendas of young people from negative to positive, from violence to non-violence, from illiteracy to education, from a lack of self-respect to a comprehensive understanding and respect for our ethnic diversities."

Lauryn figured that if she could reach disadvantaged kids during their crucial formative years, she could counteract the various negative influences that conspire to kill their spirits and rob them of their souls. By providing nurturing summer camp and after-school programs, positive role models and various educational opportunities, she knew that she could eventually improve the lives of the disenfranchised.

In May 1996, Lauryn took her first step under the auspices of the Refugee Project. While still on tour in Europe, she began orchestrating a free concert in Harlem. The idea was to bring world-class acts to people who ordinarily couldn't afford concert shows. Of course, there was more to it than that. The purpose behind the whole event was to promote voter registration in the notoriously remiss African-American community.

Within a month's time, Lauryn had secured the participation of the Wu-Tang Clan, Sean "Puffy" Combs, and the Notorious B.I.G. She'd also raised $200,000 to stage the event that she called Hoodshock. The amazing thing was not that 10,000 people turned out to witness the happening but that it happened at all. When Lauryn first brought up the idea, the consensus was that the plan was destined for certain failure. "Everyone said we couldn't do it," Suzette Williams, treasurer of the Refugee Project, told *Essence*.

But Lauryn persevered until her efforts came to fruition. "She takes an idea and makes it happen," said Williams. "She's not scared of obstacles, she's not scared of opposition, and that's rare. Many times people will tell you you can't do something, and you just say, 'All right then, I can't do it.' But Lauryn won't stop."

When the multi-act Smokin' Grooves tour rolled around in July, *The Score* sat atop the *Billboard* pop chart and had gone platinum three times over. The summer tour was dubbed the "Black Lollapalooza" since hip-hop was to be the only genre represented. On this cross-country trek, the Fugees would be traveling with Cypress Hill, Ziggy Marley, D'Angelo, Tony Rich, and Spearhead.

In the muggy thick of July and August heat, come rain or come shine, the world-weary threesome took to the stage. This was their first taste of playing to larger crowds. While the atmosphere wasn't quite as intimate as in the smaller venues, the enthusiasm of the audience was that much more palpable. Luckily, the Fugees enjoyed the vast venue experience. It would not be their last.

Their CD just kept on selling. After those of the MTV generation all owned a copy of their very own, it was time for the VH-1 crew to get involved. Like the Energizer Bunny, it just kept selling and selling. As a result, the Fugees were pushed to keep going. They remained on the road long after the 1996 Smokin' Grooves tour was over and done with. It was a never-ending round of hotels, auditoriums, and buses. The only thing changing was the size of their expanding audiences and hotel rooms.

In their short rest periods, Lauryn, Wyclef, and Pras escaped to their families in New Jersey. Often meeting up at their Booga Basement home base, they kept their personal lives devoid of showbiz trappings. "People expect us to live in a mansion," Wyclef told *Harper's Bazaar*. "But our values are about more than just living in a nice house."

Lauryn's star entourage included no round-the-clock bodyguards, no publicist, and no army of personal assistants. She didn't have "people," she had friends. They were the same group of folks who had known her when she had come perilously close to being booed off the Apollo Theatre stage. To the rest of the world, she may have been the very picture of an untouchable star, but to her loved ones, Lauryn was the hometown kid who'd made good—just as they always knew she would.

Chapter Six

Behind the Music

In 1996, many people would have gladly changed places with one of America's most beautiful, intelligent, and talented songstresses. She seemed to have it all. To the outside world, Lauryn was a princess and her life a fairy tale. The reality, of course, was far less saccharine.

As often happens with famous musical acts, trouble was brewing in Fugee-land. Even when *The Score* was first released, Lauryn found herself unable to feel appropriately joyful over the album's success. Signs of her distraught inner state would leak out at the most inopportune moments: her eyes would well up with tears at a photo session; her facial expression would betray sadness at a festive press conference; she'd avoid the onslaught of well-wishers gathering backstage after a show. All in all, she had a hard time playing the part of hip-hop's brightest star.

While one could easily make the mistake of attributing all of Lauryn's problems to good, old-fashioned man trouble, her melancholia was the result of several factors, not the least of which was her newfound acclaim. *The Score* had reached a much wider contingent than *Blunted on Reality*. As a result, a new crop of people were now holding Lauryn up as the Fugees' saving grace. All this emphasis on the lady was again the source of some strain within the group.

Throughout the tour, especially after "Killing Me Softly" became a multiplatinum single, Lauryn felt inordinately uncomfortable being the subject of so much adulation. Wyclef and Pras were routinely pushed aside so that the fans might get a better look at their favorite rapper. As early as March 1996, at the beginning of the Fugees' tour, it was obvious whom the crowds had turned out to see. Once, when the group was arriving at a Montreal gig, Lauryn was getting so much more attention than Pras from the ticket holders at the door that a security guard actually mistook the low-profile Fugee for an interloper and attempted to deny him entry into the venue.

Needless to say, such occurrences sat none too well with the cousins. Not that they took out their disappointment on Lauryn, for, after all, none of it was her fault. If she could have deflected the tide of affection from herself onto her group mates, she would have gladly done so.

In fact, she tried her best to keep from upstaging her overlooked partners. Whether at a promotional event or at a concert, Lauryn was always walking on eggshells. She didn't want anyone mistaking her for the Fugees' lead singer. That wasn't her role, and knowing that many people thought it was made her very uneasy. "It was very important for my brothers to shine," she told *Vibe*. "And I think for a period of time, I was almost afraid to shine."

Lauryn has, in the past, described her energy as "very idealistic." Considering the way she dealt with the public's misconceptions, the description is most apt. There was nothing of the selfish media hound in Lauryn. She consistently sublimated her own wishes for the sake of her surrogate brothers. During the tour, Wyclef and Pras could pursue all the auxiliary projects they wanted. Lauryn, on the other hand, felt that she had to limit herself in order not to draw too much attention to herself.

Wyclef's extracurricular activity was truly prolific. Every chance he had, he was in someone's studio, remixing tracks. While on tour with the Fugees, he managed to find the time to work with Michael Jackson, Cypress Hill, Sublime, Simply Red, and Bounty Killer. He also recorded his own music, mostly in Creole, sending the songs along to Haitian radio stations where they immediately became Number 1 hits. His nonstop schedule even had the Fugees' manager at DAS Communications concerned over potential burnout. While Pras wasn't quite as busy, he seemed to feel just as free to do as he saw fit.

Lauryn's, of course, was a special case. While no one expected her to restrict her talents to the group, she was too worried about hurting Wyclef's and Pras's feelings to do exactly as she chose. Eventually, the guys began to rely on Lauryn's single-minded dedication to the group. To see her so committed allayed their fears. Yet, both kept right on working their own angles. In *Vibe*, Lauryn attributed their zeal for outside projects to a need for security: "Like, just in case I did jump ship, everybody else was going to be all right."

Ever the sensitive caregiver, she understood her friends and didn't begrudge them their side pursuits. If anything, she empathized with their plight a little too much. The boundaries she imposed upon her career would come back to haunt her in the future.

Lauryn managed to squeeze in a few quasi-solo ventures, such as recording "The Sweetest Thing" for the soundtrack of *Love Jones*, but the year that she spent on the road with the Fugees was marked by a near-total absence of creative activity. Although much of this slump was Lauryn's self-imposed way of compensating for her high visibility, she told *Vibe* about yet another contributing factor: "We all existed in denial for a while. But when you're in denial, you're sort of stagnant. We stayed on tour for a long time. Tour is interesting because it ain't home, which means it's not reality. It's the road."

And the road would have been absolutely unbearable if the three musicians were forever at odds. Living out of their roomy tour bus, fully equipped with miniature beds, the Fugees were constant roommates. Pras's and Wyclef's were the first faces Lauryn saw in the morning and the last ones she saw before drifting off to sleep. Thus, she often repressed her innermost thoughts and feelings to maintain a friendly group dynamic.

As one of the most honest songwriters in the business, Lauryn had always written about what was going on inside her. But since she couldn't very well craft lyrics about feelings that she was not allowing herself to examine, there was simply nothing to express. In this manner, weeks could fly by without Lauryn having written a thing.

The long series of show dates also wreaked havoc on Lauryn's vocal chords. For months on end, she would be expected to belt out "Killing Me Softly" with the same heart and soul that had gone into the record. It wasn't easy. To preserve her voice for the shows, she had to do more than drink massive quantities of hot honey water. On those days when she had to sing, she would turn herself into a virtual recluse and avoid talking to people prior to the performances. Again, this ran contrary to Lauryn's open and effusive nature.

To be fair, the tour wasn't all gloom and misery. The group had just as many good times as conflicts. Wherever the group stopped to play—New York, Toronto, Detroit, Chicago, or L.A.—they were greeted with the ultimate in fanfare. Invariably, the audiences would fall head over heels in love with the Fugees. Best of all, as any of their supporting acts could attest, the trio was still a tight-knit family unit. "We were a crazy bunch," Lauryn told *Rolling Stone*. "We used to do some wild things . . . we had a lot of fun."

All in all, the touring proved to be a wild ride. As such, it threw Lauryn completely off balance. The constant attention, the total lack of privacy, and the tremendous change in circumstance combined to form a stress-laden experience. For some time, even the clear-sighted Lauryn couldn't discern truth from illusion. As she explained to *Rolling Stone*, "When you're in the middle of a storm, it's kind of hard to see. You're just driving to get out."

In a few months' time, Lauryn had suddenly morphed into one of the most influential figures in hip-hop. She had good reason to find some satisfaction in her new status. As a smart and self-respecting black woman, she felt that she could help improve the image of females in rap: "I keep my clothes on, so I'm not emphasizing that [sexual] part of me. . . . Right now, it's popular for women to promote this really dumb, money-hungry image. It's not healthy. We can't see the effects now, but that shit is gonna be painful later."

The opportunity to change prevailing attitudes encompassed everything that Lauryn wanted to get out of fame. Many a time, however, she felt as if she were banging her head against a brick wall. Picture this: Lauryn, Wyclef, and Pras are sitting with an entertainment journalist and answering questions. Lauryn is waiting patiently to air her views on various social and political issues. Instead, something entirely different happens. She recounted this typical scene to *Showbiz*: "I remember interviews where guys would ask Pras what he thought of the African Diaspora or the state of hip-hop, and then I'd get asked about lipstick!"

Inside, Lauryn was seething. She did not graduate as one of the top students in her high school class and study at Columbia University to talk about makeup tips. She didn't stay up nights working on meaningful verses only to be complimented on her voice and her look. But that's exactly what was going on. One article after another concentrated on the talents of Wyclef and Pras, while praising Lauryn mostly for her unearthly beauty and savvy fashion sense.

If the situation hadn't been so tragically indicative of the times, it would have been laughable. In the *Washington Times*, Lauryn said that the interviews made her feel "as if my opinion didn't matter at all. And it was strange because the three of us as a group aren't like that, but I just felt relegated by the men talking shop all the time."

The unconscious chauvinism that Lauryn encountered shortly after the release of *The Score* was only a sign of things to come. Months later, when Wyclef released his solo album, *Wyclef Jean Presents the Carnival Featuring Refugee Allstars*, she would find out exactly how discriminatory the music industry could be.

As pained as she was by the media's focus on her fly appearance, the ceaseless touring, and the public's reluctance to accept Pras and Wyclef as equally valuable Fugees, none of that compared to the hurt she was experiencing in her personal life.

In a couple of unguarded moments, Lauryn spoke on record of a soured intimate relationship. Since she consistently refused to reveal any details or identify the man in question and had never been seen in public with anyone but her Fugee counterparts, rumors eventually surfaced that her romance was with Wyclef, who had been married since 1993. Despite both dismissing such reports as idle gossip (albeit without ever denying their veracity), the speculation persists to this very day.

The buzz on Lauryn's love life, however, didn't begin until some time after she'd ended the passionate but dead-end relationship. The years that she'd spent in her first all-consuming adult relationship are perhaps best described as sweet misery, a can't-live-with-him-can't-live-without-him emotional roller coaster, which would one day inspire her to pen her greatest work to date.

By April 1996, however, the affair was over, and *Essence* quoted a disconsolate Lauryn saying, "I'm a lot hurt and I'm a lot disappointed. Half of the niggas that I meet, they don't know about relationships. And when they hurt you, they don't know it. Or if they do know, they don't really give a f--- because they've been so bruised, battered and scarred themselves."

Coupled with the many stumbling blocks Lauryn encountered on the road with the Fugees, the conclusion of her long-term romance cemented her dejected state of mind. For some months after the breakup, she wasn't herself. "I'd spent so many years working at a relationship that didn't work that I was just like, 'I'm going to write these songs and pour my heart into them,' " she told *Essence*.

Unfortunately, try as she might, the words

would not come. Her packed tour schedule left no time for sorting out a heartache. Quiet contemplation would have to wait until Lauryn got done living life on the road. "With the Fugees," she told *Showbiz*, "we were constantly dashing from place to place, bus to hotel. . . . Your perspective gets stunted."

Fortunately, Lauryn still had her family to rely on. Even though she could no longer be with them every day, she stayed in constant touch over the phone. Nothing cheered Lauryn's spirits like a good, long talk with her mom. "I would say these pessimistic things to my mother, and she'd be like, 'Oh, girl, you'd think you were forty-seven.' "

But Lauryn actually had good reason to fear for her heart. As she explained to *Vibe*, "If you're a man in the music business, there's girls throwing their panties at you. And you can either accept it or reject it, and most of the time they accept it because they've never had that much overwhelming attention in their lives. For women in the music business, it's very different. Men are often intimidated by you, or they're crazy. So it's not easy to make connections with real people."

Lauryn decided that she'd kissed enough frogs to last a lifetime. She threw herself into her work and into her humanitarian pursuits. By the summer of 1996, she had effectively resigned herself to living solo—at least for the time being. Little did she know that her prince was waiting just around the corner.

If anyone other than God can be credited with turning Lauryn's life around, that person would surely be Rohan Marley. The son of reggae legend Bob Marley, twenty-four-year-old Rohan had come out to watch the Fugees' show. On *The Score*, the group had covered his father's inimitable "No Woman No Cry" to perfection. He must have liked the way they played the song in concert as well, because no sooner had the show ended than Rohan was backstage and looking to speak with Lauryn. In *Essence*, she recalled her first impression of the dread-locked Rasta-man: "He said, 'Hey. Hey, I like you. I want to talk to you.' "

She couldn't very well refuse to give Rohan the time of day. The former University of Miami football player was, after all, the son of one of Lauryn's all-time greatest idols. Before he passed away in 1981, Bob Marley had brought hope to millions of people in every corner of the globe, Lauryn included. His music continued to inspire her songs, and the least she could do was talk to her hero's son.

One problem: Lauryn was still on the rebound. Well aware of her own vulnerable state, she wasn't about to set herself up for another fall. The injuries she'd sustained while being head over heels in love still smarted, and the last thing she needed now was to get swept off her feet again. "I wasn't really checking for anybody," she said. "I was very much into my music."

Lauryn drew the line, declining Rohan's invitations. But he would not be so easily put off. The man simply wouldn't take no for an answer. He was determined to go out with her and get to know her better. The early stage of their courtship was the epitome of the classic mating dance: him coming around to woo, her sending him away. Rohan was just the kind of deeply spiritual and profoundly secure person who could laugh in the face of repeated rejection. Soon, Lauryn realized that she'd found a worthy match in Rohan.

She relented. The relationship started off slow, with friendly conversations and decidedly low-key dates. With very little drama and a whole lot of stability, Rohan was slowly but surely winning Lauryn over. On the whole, this was the antithesis of her past romances. Instead of feeling crazy and out of control, Lauryn's new boyfriend made her feel safe and cared for. Three years ago, she might have thumbed her nose at someone as solid as Rohan, but as she explained to *Details*, "I encountered the truth, and the truth was a lot more moderate than 'Oh, darling, I would run to the mountains and seas for you.' "

The new man in her life could actually back

up his professions of love with action. That uncommon quality alone was enough to make Lauryn's heart swell with affection. She'd had enough of bad boys who, as she put it, "talk hard, love hard and when you try to leave they do silly things like cut themselves." Finding that the change of pace agreed with her, she forsook all others and committed herself to Rohan.

Just as Lauryn was beginning to feel something akin to satisfaction, she was felled by a bomb that seemed to come out of nowhere. The summer of 1996 brought Rohan into her life, but it also brought its share of controversy. Suddenly, the peace-loving Lauryn Hill found herself having to contend with charges of racism.

The news hit her like a ton of bricks. A random caller to shock jock Howard Stern's radio show claimed that he'd heard Lauryn telling MTV that she would never have made *The Score* if she'd known that so many white people would be buying it. The allegation had no basis in fact whatsoever. Even the people at MTV denied ever hearing such a statement pass Lauryn's lips. Simply put, Lauryn never said anything of the sort.

Yet hundreds of thousands of listeners had heard the caller, and had believed him. They passed the story on to their friends, and the rumor just kept on snowballing. Lauryn was horrified as well as infuriated. The thought that someone could slander her with such wanton disregard for truth or consequences was shocking. And make no mistake, there were consequences. "From this one broadcast," she told *Teen People*, "all of a sudden people who appreciated my music thought that there was something wrong with who I was and what I represented."

It was all so preposterous. How anyone who'd listened to her music could ever mistake her for a racist was a complete mystery to Lauryn. To extinguish the rumor, she went to the source of the problem. She called a radio station and said, "How can I possibly be a racist? My music is universal music. And I believe in God. If I believe in God, then I have to love all of God's creations. There can be no segregation."

Of course, this was the type of rumor that no number of denials could squelch. Most people never got wind of the ugly incident. Others heard her refute the story as a vicious lie and promptly forgot about it. Still others, however, never learned of Lauryn's response and continue to insist that they'd heard her saying those vile things on MTV with their own ears. To this day, Lauryn sticks by her story. "I am not a racist," she recently told *Teen People*. "There's nothing racist about anything in my heart."

* * *

All combined, the heartbreak, the never-ending tour schedule, and the public's misconceptions of her personal beliefs—as well as her role in the Fugees—were enough to put a damper on the year that should have been Lauryn's greatest triumph thus far. Had it not been for her family and Rohan, Lauryn might have found herself a bitterly disillusioned twenty-one-year-old.

But as she and Rohan grew closer, Lauryn grew happier. The relationship progressed at such a rapid pace that in January 1997, Lauryn learned that she was with child. The news, coming as it did right around the time that the Grammy nominations were handed down, left Lauryn feeling conflicted: If she chose to carry the pregnancy to term, her career, now at its zenith, might never recover.

Certainly, the recognition from the National Academy of Recording Arts and Sciences (NARAS) marked an all-time career high for Lauryn and her Fugee allies. In February 1997, the group made its first appearance at the Grammy Awards ceremony. The nominations, however, weren't the only exciting aspect of the gala event. The trio had also been asked to perform.

With an estimated 1.5 billion people tuning in worldwide, the Grammy performance provided the group with the perfect opportunity to disseminate their message. Those who caught their act saw Wyclef brandishing the Haitian flag and proclaiming his cultural pride to one and all. They may have been one of the most popular groups in the world, but the Fugees were still a band of refugees trying to make a point—that all people who are on the outside looking in should be valued for their unique perspectives.

Wyclef, Pras, and Lauryn came home from the show wielding two trophies, one for *The Score*, which garnered the Best Rap Album honor, and the other for "Killing Me Softly with His Song," which was acknowledged as the Best R&B Performance by a Duo or Group. But even as Lauryn accepted her just rewards, thoughts of her unborn child must have been uppermost on her mind.

She was truly at an impasse. While many women in her position would have been quick to terminate the pregnancy, Lauryn wasn't so sure. She'd already seen what fame had to offer. It had been her dream, but she knew life had more to offer. "I mean, after you do so much at a young age, you start to realize it's not about doing so much," she explained to *Vibe*. "I have so many friends and associates who say 'I wanna be a singer, I wanna do this and that.' And I say 'Please don't let that be your final goal in life 'cause you'll be so disappointed.' "

Still uncertain as to how she should proceed, Lauryn turned to her family and friends for advice. She already knew how Rohan felt; he

113

would support her no matter what she decided. Her family turned out to be equally sympathetic. Valerie even offered to help Lauryn care for the baby once it arrived.

Yet, there were those who considered motherhood on par with career suicide. "A lot of people said, 'Girl, you've got a career. Don't be having no baby now.' I looked at myself in the mirror and I said, 'Okay, this is a hard one,' and I prayed on it," she recalled in *Essence*. "In my brain I said, 'I'm okay financially. I have a man in my life who loves me. I have a supportive family. I believe I would be a good mother.' I said, 'Wow, the only reason for me not to have this child is because it would inconvenience me.' And that wasn't a strong enough argument for me. . . ."

She could not argue with the soundness of her own logic. Although she and Rohan were not yet married, they agreed to raise the baby together. It was a joyous occasion and things were definitely looking up. Of course, the media still hadn't a clue about Lauryn's impending motherhood. She was determined and content to keep the baby, as well as her relationship with Rohan, a secret for as long as possible.

Lauryn was glad to see her un-
partner making his bid for
cording to music industry wis-
embers of Fugee-caliber ensem-
strike out on their own, it can
e thing: the end of the group is
e of external speculation can take
act, as fellow group members begin
industry's rumblings and start to
hat if?" No such fears plagued the
owever. Tighter than most groups,
d Pras understood Wyclef's need for
ession only too well.

ng after the Grammys, Lauryn had to
the strength to accompany the Fugees
another tour abroad. They returned
pe, where they played arenas and sta-
. The great swarms of fans were a sight to
d. Never had a hip-hop group received
magnificent props either at home or
ad. But the Fugees weren't just any hip-hop
up: They were the number one act in the
rld. As such, they felt the need to make a
eeping statement. Wyclef's idea was to round
ff the world tour in his hometown of Port-au-
rince, Haiti. The past year had seen the Fugees
trotting the globe and slaying audiences left
and right. Wyclef had come a long way, but he
had yet to come full circle.

Of course, he wanted much more than the
superficial pleasure of returning to his birth-

118

Chapter Seven

Life Goes On

Pleased as she was with her nascent Grammy
collection, Lauryn wasn't at all surprised that
her group had been thus honored. The album
had sold so fast for so long that by the time
sales tapered off, nearly 18 million homes
worldwide were equipped with their very own
copy. Throughout the history of rap, there had
never been anything like it. A monster seller
such as *The Score* comes around with all the fre-
quency of a leap year. It is exactly the type of
record that the music industry prays for and is
quick to reward come Grammy season.

The album made Lauryn a very rich young
woman. Yet she would never be a contender for
a *Lifestyles of the Rich and Famous* episode.
While her net worth was definitely the stuff of
champagne wishes and caviar dreams, she remained a stalwart devotee of soul food and
home cooking. Her millions stayed in South Orange, New Jersey. Aside from indulging her
taste for fashion, she outfitted her parents with

115

a spacious, three-story brick house in an up-scale area of South Orange. After helping Valerie and Mal move in, Lauryn and Rohan set up shop in her childhood home, located only five minutes away from her parents' new digs.

All of it was preparation for the baby's arrival. Charged with the task of child rearing, Lauryn's priorities fell into place as if by magic. Even while she was being hailed as the queen of hip-hop, her only concern was to grow as a person and become a good mother for her child.

It would have been very easy for Lauryn to go totally glam. She could have bought a large penthouse in Manhattan or gone Hollywood like so many other music industry insiders, but that kind of life would have rung a false note for her. "Jersey may not have the nightlife of New York City, but it's very flavorful," she told *Details*. "It's about the communal vibe, the old man sitting on the stoop outside. And this is the place where I *started*—so the same fire I had originally is the one I maintain when I'm here. And when it comes to hip-hop, it's very important to stay in touch with who you are, so I probably won't ever move very far away."

Staying grounded and keeping some sense of normalcy in her hectic life was of the utmost importance. Lauryn had seen plenty of entertainers who'd let success go to their heads, and she wasn't planning on joining their ranks. "I have about thirty plaques that stay in one

closet," sh
where the
a travesty!"
time, becaus
placent like th
or my success
happy just bein'

Only a year ago,
a lost love. And all t.
singles in the world
fact. But since Rohan
those unhappy days see
years away. "Ro came in
time that I wasn't looking
the exact time that I nee
badly," Lauryn said in *Rollin*
his heart on his sleeve in this
that's where I put my heart, so w

Her career and personal life on t
was a changed woman. She now ha
tude to tackle her Fugee duties with
site vigor. While still in her first trime
began assisting Wyclef in the studio.
hard at work on his first solo venture,
Jean Presents the Carnival Featuring Refugee
stars. She sang on a few of his tracks and ev
lent a hand as a producer.

The Carnival was recorded at Wyclef's new home studio in Midtown Manhattan between

place in a blaze of glory. If his group's visit couldn't be of help to anyone, what was the point? That's why the Fugees agreed to make their show a benefit concert. All the proceeds would be donated to the neediest of Haitians: the orphaned children, the starving artists, and the homeless refugees who had been denied asylum by the Dominican Republic. But since all the benefit concerts in the world could not help a country that was unwilling to help itself, the trio's primary hope was that their show would give the people a sense of cultural and national pride.

After extensive planning with Haitian officials, it was decided that the group would fly to Haiti on April 9, 1997. Since this was not a typical concert, Lauryn, Wyclef, and Pras intended to stay in the country for a few days. This way, they would be able to participate in a number of events and Pras and Lauryn could get a feel for the land and its people. For the Haitians, the Fugees' arrival was nothing short of a national holiday. "They treated us like we were the Pope," Wyclef told the Newark *Star-Ledger*. "When we were there, the whole country stopped. There was no work, no school, nothing. The Fugees were in town."

Wyclef had become a hero in his homeland. His constant efforts on behalf of the Haitian people, both at the Grammy Awards and in the recording studio, had not gone unnoticed. The fact that he'd consistently written songs in Creole and sent them to Haiti's radio stations free of charge inspired his many Haitian fans with a great love for the Fugees. As befitted the conquering heroes, the group was honored at the Presidential Palace and received a key to the city of Port-au-Prince.

After following through on their packed itinerary, the trio was ready for the main event. With several local favorites also scheduled to perform, the outdoor concert was slated to last six hours and draw a mammoth crowd. With an estimated 80,000 people in attendance, the usually bustling streets of Port-au-Prince must have seemed eerily empty the day the Fugees took to the stage.

Never before had the group played before such a large audience. The outpouring of affection warmed their hearts and strengthened their resolve. Rising to the occasion, the Fugees played for hours. It was the longest and most adrenaline-charged performance of their career. Wyclef had kicked off the festivities by revealing his motives to the expectant mass, saying, "This is the chance for people to see that Haiti is a civilized country." As if to cooperate with their champion, the fans ensured that the show went off without a hitch. The night was capped by an elaborate fireworks display—a sight which the awestruck Haitians had not seen in quite a few years.

* * *

Infamous for its violence, poverty, political unrest, and high incidence of AIDS, Haiti was truly in dire need of an image makeover. But it was also in need of the funds generated by the show. At the end of their performance, the Fugees were about to descend the stage when Wyclef grabbed the mike. "Tomorrow, I'll be on a plane back to New York. Watch where the money goes," he warned.

In light of Haiti's rampant bureaucratic corruption, Wyclef had every reason to caution the public. The events that followed on the heels of the concert proved he'd been right. Eighty thousand people had paid to see the Fugees play, and the performance had grossed $300,000. Anywhere else, a show of such grandeur would have translated into a financial bonanza. But according to Haitian officials, the concert was more of a drain on the country's resources than a boon. Citing expenses such as hotel rooms, the officials claimed that not only had the show not turned a profit but that it had actually cost more than it earned.

Although an official inquiry followed, there was not enough evidence to confirm the Fugees' suspicions of embezzlement and misappropriation. "The government could do something like that," Wyclef told *Vibe*, "and no one could prove anything."

In response to the disheartening news, Wyclef

put out a statement of his own: "Having been given a chance to perform a concert for the Haitian people was a dream come true for us. The purpose of our trip to Haiti was to give a great show for the people of Haiti, to send out a positive image of Haiti and its people to the world and to raise money for several worthy charitable organizations in Haiti."

Obviously, he would have to think of another way to help his people. Having failed to accomplish one of the key objectives in Haiti, Wyclef set up the Wyclef Jean Foundation, intending to stage additional benefit concerts "where we can have compete control over, and full knowledge of, all revenues and expenses."

Despite his generous humanitarian efforts, Wyclef knew that his ultimate gift to his motherland lay in making music. Through his solo album, *The Carnival*, he wished to introduce Americans to Haitian and Caribbean culture. Wise to the ways of hip-hop, he left the Creole songs for last. "I figure you start off in Newark or somewhere on the East Coast if you want to draw the hip-hop kids into the album," he told the *Star-Ledger*. "You get them feeling like it's a dope album before they get to the Creole stuff. You want them to get down with the [Creole] culture, but you have to give them what they're used to."

The ploy worked. Released in June 1997, *The Carnival* became a smash hit of the platinum-plus variety. The critics liked it as well, often citing the album as one of the year's ten best. In the blink of an eye, Wyclef went from being one of the guys backing up Lauryn Hill to the mastermind of the entire Fugee operation in the public's eye.

While her group mate reveled in the friendly glow of the spotlight, Lauryn was doing all she could to bear up under the weight of the media's gaze. News of her pregnancy had taken her fans off guard. Lauryn Hill, an unwed mother at twenty-two? Her image as a strong and intelligent role model for young African-American women was suddenly in peril.

Even as Lauryn tried to keep her steadily expanding proportions under wraps, there were those gossip hounds who would not be denied. During one radio interview with Wendy Williams, Lauryn was shocked to find herself in the hot seat. The nosy DJ simply refused to accept "No comment" as an answer. She had to know, was Lauryn pregnant? "I know this is your job," Lauryn responded, "but this is my life." Lauryn recalled that interview in *Vibe*, explaining how she'd been "in the woman's face and there was no compassion whatsoever. But people who show no compassion will be shown no compassion."

Of course, after that incident, the whole music business was abuzz with news of the young Ms. Hill's out-of-wedlock conception. Since she could still hide the signs of the impending birth, Lauryn declined to discuss the matter with anyone from the mass media. But when MTV's Tabitha Soren tried to get Lauryn to open up, she finally relented.

"Are you with child?" Soren asked, as a surprised Lauryn burst into uncomfortable laughter.

"Don't blush on me now," Soren insisted.

"Actually, yes. Yes, I am," Lauryn replied.

That was it. The baby was now common knowledge. But the name of the father was not. Since Rohan and Lauryn had kept such a low profile, rumors of an illicit affair with Wyclef began to pop up in the most unlikely places. Even reputable news syndicates erroneously named Wyclef as Lauryn's boyfriend and her baby's father.

To be fair, Lauryn's halfhearted denials of a onetime relationship with Wyclef did leave some room for doubt. Whenever she was asked about the rumored affair, she would sidestep the question with answers such as the one she gave *Vibe*: "All of us in the group were very close. I don't have a response to that one. We were a dynamic group in the sense that we grew up together. So there will be a lot of love there."

Feeling that she had a right to her privacy, Lauryn ignored the inquisition. She knew that people would find out about Rohan eventually, and the public outcry would then die down. In the meanwhile, she wanted to enjoy every moment of her secret love. "I felt like the world had enough of me," she told *Harper's Bazaar.* "I felt like I put my soul on records, and I didn't have to answer any global question about who my boyfriend was."

Although she tried to keep her personal affairs private, Lauryn was absolutely forthright with her closest colleagues. Whereas Rohan and her family had encouraged Lauryn to follow her heart, those on the inside of the music business had responded with a resounding "nay." Apparently, to them, pop stardom and motherhood had all the melding properties of oil and water. Even Lauryn's beloved musical role models could offer little in the way of affirmation. "I had a conversation with Nina Simone, and she said, 'Lauryn, I don't think that a woman can have a family and be in the music business,' " she told *Spin.* "It was a heavy thing."

Despite the near-universal disapproval, Lauryn was undeterred. While the criticism of the artistic community was certainly troubling, she had already pledged herself to her unborn child. Taking solace in Rohan and her mother, Lauryn knew that she would find a way to outwit the rigid system and have it all. "I made a commitment to music *and* family a long time ago," she later explained to *Details,* "and my theory on why I'm having children so young is because my mother's still young and strapping, and there's nobody else that I'd trust with my kids but her and their dad."

In the seventh month of her pregnancy, Lauryn had no choice but to take a leave from the Fugees. Up until that time, she had been "very content" to be a part of the group. She had been so involved in the proceedings, so desperate to make things work for the trio, that she had not stopped to think about the possible repercussions. Now that she had time to reflect, Lauryn told *Vibe* that she "was able to watch Wyclef and everything that went on from the outside in."

Watching Wyclef, or at least the public's response to Wyclef's *The Carnival*, cleared up any illusions Lauryn may have had about the music business. Throughout her career, she had turned down lucrative offers because she believed in "all for one, and one for all." But the summer of 1997 would bring an end to that particular fantasy.

Initially, Lauryn was thrilled to see Wyclef prospering on his own. She had never questioned his talent and always denied the charge that he was riding on her coattails. She eagerly anticipated the release of *The Carnival* and foresaw no downside to the success of her group mate.

Unfortunately, the artistic triumph of Wyclef's first solo album came with a dark side. Although

Lauryn loved the acclaim heaped upon her all-too-deserving partner, the media's references to Wyclef's dominant role in forging the Fugees' sound made her cringe. "I remember seeing the publicity and the energy go from like, 'You thought the girl was all that? Here's the guy who really sings.' I was just like, 'Whaaaat?' " Lauryn recalled in *Vibe*. "I said, 'Okay, have I been stagnant for the sake of promoting this "group collective effort"?' I was so busy trying to convince the world of how strong we were as a unit."

Still a relative newcomer to the business, Lauryn couldn't have known that where musical alliances are concerned, one partner's gain could mean another's loss. It was hard to believe that the same people who had put her up on a pedestal were now trying their hardest to knock her off. The experience opened her eyes to the grim reality of being a celebrity. All the applause, rave reviews, and adulation had had little to do with who she was as an artist.

Suddenly, the consensus was that Lauryn's role in the Fugees had not extended beyond her voice. As she explained to *Horizon Magazine*, "I think a lot of people saw the success, particularly after Wyclef's album, of the Fugees being one that was collaborative between Wyclef and myself. Him on the production, me on the vocals."

The newly formed popular opinion failed to

do justice to Lauryn's position in the Fugees. She had always been much more than the group's resident songstress. Lauryn had, after all, been coexecutive producer and cowriter of *The Score*, alongside Wyclef and Pras. Lauryn now realized that the time had come to stake her own claim.

Lauryn's creative renaissance had less to do with the spirit of friendly competition than with the impact of her pregnancy. Physical changes alone had her scurrying for the nearest writing utensil to commit her thoughts to paper. "When some women are pregnant, their hair and their nails grow," she told *Ebony*. "My mind and ability to create expanded. I had the desire to write in a capacity that I hadn't done in a while. I don't know if it's a hormonal or emotional thing. . . . I was very much in touch with my feelings at the time."

This renewed self-awareness informed her work in a way that rivalry never could. Instead of seeking increased fame and recognition, Lauryn sought only to express herself. As if to underscore the point, she wrote all her songs for other singers. There were so many artists with whom she wanted to collaborate—and so many feelings she felt compelled to express. "I had so much energy," she told *Harper's Bazaar*, "I was bouncing off the walls."

A few months earlier, she might have balked

at the notion of taking an independent step and fueling talk of a Fugees rupture, but now that she'd had some time to herself, she realized the error of her ways. Where were Wyclef and Pras now that Lauryn was in need of her friends? While her stock was up, she had been the first to cut herself down to size, refusing to leave the group and restricting her outside pursuits. Neither of her group mates seemed to share her concerns. Both cousins were off participating in high-profile collaborations, leaving Lauryn to her own devices during her last trimester. Thinking back to all the sacrifices she'd made for the sake of the group, her fellow Fugees' seemingly callous disregard was hard to stomach.

Of course, Lauryn had never been one to sit on the sidelines letting life pass her by. Thus, she gave little energy to fuming over the somewhat self-absorbed antics of Wyclef and Pras. With her delivery date just around the corner, Lauryn wrote dozens of songs, telling *Billboard*, "Every time I got hurt, every time I was disappointed, every time I learned, I just wrote a song."

She also entered into negotiations with two of her childhood idols, Queen of Soul Aretha Franklin and gospel legend CeCe Winans. For the latter, Lauryn composed a track entitled "On That Day." While the ballad isn't what one would call hip-hop standard fare, Winans's enthusiasm for the song proved that Lauryn's talent surpassed the artificial boundaries separating one musical genre from the next.

Her work with Winans also showed Lauryn to be a deft producer. Not content to hand over her brainchild with no strings attached, she insisted on seeing the project through to completion. Since few female musicians have been interested in the sound board, many viewed Lauryn's insistence on taking the producer's reins as odd. In light of Wyclef's latest outing, some even doubted Lauryn's ability to work the controls. "I guess people figure [producing] is something that women don't really know about. But I was already a legitimate producer," she said in *Essence*, referring to her work on *The Score*. "It's just that my name was totally ignored because it was beside a man's."

Even Chris Swartz, CEO of Ruffhouse, lamented the slights dealt out to the lady Fugee after *The Carnival* was released. "I don't think a lot of people gave Lauryn credit for how much she contributed to *The Score*," Swartz told the *Los Angeles Times*. "A lot of people assumed that she was just a singer."

This prevailing perception also nearly ruined Lauryn's chances of working with Aretha Franklin. Having written "A Rose Is Still a Rose" with Aretha Franklin in mind, Lauryn wanted nothing so much as to see it on the Queen of Soul's next album. But Drew Dixon, an A&R rep at Franklin's record company, Arista Records, told

Spin that it was "a hard sell getting people to believe that this twenty-three-year-old African-American woman best known for singing the hell out of [the Fugees'] 'Killing Me Softly' cover is also a really talented writer and producer."

Tenacious as ever, Lauryn maintained that she was the best person for the job. To work with CeCe Winans and Aretha Franklin were two of her lifelong dreams, and she wasn't about to let a misunderstanding stand in the way. "Even after selling [seventeen] million records, I still have to convince people that I'm a self-contained unit," she griped to *Vibe*.

Nothing, not even her fast approaching due date, could sway Lauryn from her career path. Finally, the news came in. She would indeed be producing the tracks she'd composed for both Winans and Franklin. Lauryn couldn't have been happier. The fact that she'd be serving as the producer on tunes she'd inked for legends such as Winans and Franklin assured her that, come what may, she could find work as a songwriter/producer in the future.

In August 1997, she entered the studio with CeCe Winans, who was working on her new album, *Everlasting Love*. The experience was just as electrifying as she had hoped it would be. Lauryn still remembers the recording session as if it were yesterday. "We were in the studio together, singing and dancing to a song I wrote called 'On That Day,' " she relayed to *Harper's*

Bazaar, "and the very next day my little man showed up."

While the memory of her work with CeCe Winans may one day retreat into the recesses of Lauryn's mind, she will never forget the day her son came into the world. Aside from her immediate family, Lauryn was surrounded by a veritable United Nations of caregivers. Her Jewish obstetrician, her Jamaican midwife, and her Senegalese assistant, Dieynaba, were all at her bedside with words of encouragement. She played out the delivery room scene for *Essence*, saying, "My doctor had this really strong accent. He's from Israel. And Dieynaba has a very West African–French accent. So my mother was like, 'Girl, push! C'mon, girl, push!' And Dieynaba was like, 'Push, dah'ling. Oh, push, dah'ling, push.' And my Jamaican midwife was like, 'Push, gal! Yuh ha fi push it out! Push, push!' And the doctor was totally nonchalant like, 'Oh, push, push, push.' It was hilarious!"

The joy of giving birth was like nothing Lauryn had ever known before. Looking at her newborn son, she knew that she'd made the right decision by ignoring the critics. "What began as something dark," she explained to Sonic Net, "became the brightest and most important thing to me."

The name she and Rohan chose to bestow upon the new arrival spoke volumes about the effect the baby would have on Lauryn's life. They named him after Zion, the Biblical promised land. "Names wouldn't come when I was getting ready to have him," she told *Vibe*. "The only name that came to me was Zion. I was like, 'Is Zion too much of a weight to carry?' But this little boy, man. I would say he personally delivered me from emotional and spiritual drought. He just replenished my newness. When he was born, I almost felt like I was born again."

Chapter Eight

A New Beginning

After Zion's birth was announced, many thought that the true identity of the baby's father would be forthcoming. Lauryn, however, didn't see any reason to spill the beans just yet. And who, aside from legions of curious fans, could blame her? As she explained to *Entertainment Weekly*, "I didn't feel a need to go out and do a press conference on who my child's father was."

Instead of fretting over how best to spin her motherhood in a public relations campaign, Lauryn chose to concentrate on her family and her work. Scheduled to produce the title cut of Aretha Franklin's *A Rose Is Still a Rose* album in the fall, she was content to while away the interim in South Orange, where she basked in the warmth of the family fold. While Valerie and Rohan proved to be of most help with the precious little charge, countless relations routinely dropped by to welcome the baby into their midst.

134

The Refugee Project she had founded a year earlier was still going strong. In fact, it now boasted a board of trustees featuring such illustrious names as Busta Rhymes, Mariah Carey, Sean "Puffy" Combs, D'Angelo, Spike Lee, and fellow Fugee Wyclef. In the last lazy, hazy days of summer, Lauryn found ample opportunity to attend barbecues and a whole variety of events to benefit children. As she told *People*, "I'm always on my toes. I'm always moving. I'm never still."

At length, the moment she'd been waiting for had arrived. It was time to fly to Detroit and meet Aretha Franklin. Unwilling to let Zion out of her sight so soon, Lauryn asked her mother to come along and watch the baby. A die-hard Aretha fan, Valerie didn't need to be asked twice. All anticipation, the happy threesome descended upon the Motor City ready to shake hands with the Queen of Soul. "It was amazing," Lauryn told the *Illinois Entertainer*. "I had this funny feeling like, 'I ain't supposed to be here!' I mean I grew up listening to her and it was very exciting."

While Lauryn had nothing but the utmost respect for the woman who coined the phrase R-E-S-P-E-C-T, she never expected Aretha Franklin to pick up on the hip-hop rhythm that she'd worked into "A Rose Is Still a Rose." The old-school diva's quick mastery of the song was just one of the surprises that lay in store for Lauryn. While working in Detroit, she also learned a thing or two about the history of women in production.

Franklin asked Lauryn why she'd been so keen on producing the song. Lauryn recounted the exchange that followed in *Horizon Magazine*: "She asked me why I decided to produce. And that in itself is an interesting question, because it is not a question that's usually geared towards men. It's like, 'Oh he's a producer. Okay nice to meet you, let's start to work.' So she asked me, and I started to laugh. I told her my vision and the sound that was within me was so clear, to me it would become diluted if I had to explain it to somebody, and articulate it to somebody. So it was just easier for me to do it myself. She came back to me and said, 'You know what? It was the same thing with me and [Atlantic Records exec] Jerry Wexler. But he always got the credit.' And I just started laughing. I was like, wow, this isn't a brand-new thing."

For her part, Aretha Franklin also found herself taken aback by the pulled-together young woman who oversaw her work in the recording studio. Once the track had been cut, Franklin confirmed her appreciation for Lauryn by asking her to direct the accompanying music video. "She's positive, detailed, conscientious. Frankly, I was surprised to see that in such a young woman," Franklin told *Harper's Bazaar*, positing that Lauryn might well be "an old soul." In *People*, she again spoke highly of her young collaborator, saying that "Lauryn saw the project through from A to Z, and at midnight she was still on her feet working."

Driving to the airport, Lauryn had to make one last stop while she still had the chance. As traveled as she'd become during her years with the Fugees, and as many times as she'd performed in Detroit, she had never had the time to visit the historic Motown Museum. The unassuming two-story house was the birthplace of Berry Gordy's Motown legacy, the source of Lauryn's love for music. In *Time*, she recalled walking through the museum's hallowed halls: "It was incredible to me and really inspiring."

Apparently, the site visit provided Lauryn with the very impetus she needed to tackle her greatest challenge. Like Stevie Wonder and Marvin Gaye before her, she also wanted to make music that would stand the test of time. Writing, producing, and arranging for other performers was all well and good, but it could not take the place of her true calling. Lauryn was a singer at heart, and she returned to New Jersey determined to perform her own music.

Many of the songs that would eventually find their way onto Lauryn Hill's first solo album had already been written by the time she decided to enter the studio on her own.

"Ex-Factor," for example, had originally been intended for a rock band. "I even wrote it in a higher key for another singer," she confided to *Rolling Stone*, "and it had this wailing guitar solo at the end."

The personal nature of the song was her first tip-off that she was meant to sing it herself. Having written music for musical acts ranging from hip-hop to gospel to R&B, Lauryn brought all of these influences to bear upon her album. While it was her early exposure to the classics of soul—via her mother's collection of 45s—that had given her her desire to achieve this dream, it was her recent work with Aretha Franklin and CeCe Winans that gave her the confidence to follow through.

"I was thinking that hip-hop and R&B as we now know them aren't as personal and intimate as the music I want to make," she told *Spin*. But changing the situation did not promise to be easy. How, Lauryn wondered, would kids raised on sampling take to her honest, homespun approach to music making? "I was nervous that people weren't going to be able to relate," she admitted.

The fact that Lauryn flat out hated what she saw going on in the music industry considerably strengthened her resolve. Armed with a cache of very fixed ideas on the state of contemporary music, she set out to make a change. "Once I had my child, I was forced to sit still.

Had I not sat still, maybe I would have been caught up in the whirlwind, too. But because I was on the outside, I could see just how materialistic the industry was," she told *Rolling Stone*. "It frustrated me that it had nothing to do with talent and musical merit. MCs didn't have to write their rhymes; singers didn't really have to be able to sing. I just felt like the world of music was upside down."

Finding herself caught in the middle of the age-old quality versus quantity debate, Lauryn sided with the former. Instead of writing songs for mass consumption, she wanted to touch the hearts of her listeners. Her best defense against falling into the hit-making abyss was her superstar status. Much as she resented the unreasonable expectations that came with stardom, she knew that she had only her fame to thank for her leverage. As she told *Pulse!*, "I was blessed that I had been successful with the Fugees, so I had a platform to come out as a [solo] artist with a little more power and creative control."

As any creator of a small album knows, record companies are only too happy to run a successful formula into the ground. Try to do something different, however, and the record execs' smiles immediately disappear into thin air. Lauryn's case was no exception. "Making the music was easy," she told *Girl* magazine. "What was tough was convincing people to believe in a departure from the norm. I think people wanted me to do 'Killing Me Softly' part 3. But I wanted to do something different. So, I stuck to my soul and shot from the heart."

Ruffhouse Records CEO Chris Swartz concurred with Lauryn's assessment, telling *Entertainment Weekly*, "Everybody probably expected her to have Puffy Combs, Teddy Riley, Babyface, all the top-line, marquee R&B producers on there. Instead, she chose to do it herself and to make a very introspective, retro kind of record using live musicians."

Granted, Swartz himself was not altogether sure where Lauryn was going with her first solo effort. But he wasn't about to tell a multiplatinum recording artist how to run her business. "I had total control," Lauryn told *Horizon Magazine*. "Chris Swartz at Ruffhouse, my label, said, 'Listen, you have never done anything stupid thus far, so let me let you do your thing.' I'm sure everybody was skeptical . . . but this was something I wanted to do separate to the entire sound. I didn't want to come out with a Rufugee All-Stars type of sound. I wanted to come out with something that was uniquely and very clearly a Lauryn Hill album."

Lauryn's decision to produce her own album met with a fair share of raised eyebrows. While some wondered why she was choosing to exclude her Fugee friends from the recording process, others simply refused to believe that anything good could come from a female producer. Despite the wave of skepticism, there wasn't a doubt in Lauryn's mind that she was doing the right thing. "Hey, it's my album," she told *Harper's Bazaar*. "Who else can tell my story better than me?"

She was still toying with the notion of inviting her in-demand group mate Wyclef into the studio at some later date, but Lauryn resolved to give her own capabilities a fair shake before calling for reinforcements. Wyclef, however, was certain that Lauryn would indeed be requesting his services. "She'll just bring me in at the end," he told the Newark *Star-Ledger*. "I'm there to support her if she needs me to."

Of course, Lauryn would never make that call. The subject matter would prove much too personal to be tackled by anyone other than herself. As she explained to Planet Sound, "I can hardly say: Hey, Pras, I've written a song about my son. Wanna rock a verse on that one?!" And while she may have had some initial minor insecurities about her abilities to bring the record together, they vanished as soon as her work got under way. Her very first act was to corral a support network. "I surrounded myself with a very strong team of people," she told *Pulse!*, "my A&R person, Suzette Williams, my management . . . my family and close friends, people who could protect my vision."

As far as going to the Fugees' management, DAS Communications, was concerned, Lauryn wasn't interested. Deciding that only her most intimate relations had her best interests at heart, she chose to empower them with the managerial responsibilities. David Sonenberg, president of DAS Communications, was justly miffed by the news, but considering that the Fugees were his biggest clients, he was all diplomacy. "I want her to be happy and successful in both her individual career and her career with the Fugees," Sonenberg told the *Los Angeles Times*. "I wish she felt that there wasn't a conflict, but I'm prepared to try to work things out so that she can move ahead with another manager in the solo arena."

Thus, Lauryn's solo outing was independent in every sense of the word. Aside from staying with the same record label, Lauryn cut every string that connected her with the Fugees to record the album that she would call *The Miseducation of Lauryn Hill*. While the title had ties to Carter G. Woodson's book *The Mis-Education of the Negro*, Lauryn elaborated upon the personal meaning of the name on Sonic Net: "It's really about the things that you've learned outside of school, outside of what society deems appropriate and mandatory. I have a lot of respect for academia. . . . But there was a lot that I had to learn, life lessons, that wasn't part of any scholastic curriculum. It's really our passage into adulthood, when we leave that place of idealism and naïveté."

In other words, the whole album was to be a sketch of the artist's coming of age. In creating a work that was so resolutely, unabashedly autobiographical, she was bucking the system that valued posturing over candor and money over integrity. She vowed to tell the truth and nothing but the truth. Drawing her insight and inspiration from the Bible, Lauryn thanked God for helping her to see her way clear of the many distractions and temptations inherent in the music business.

Now was Lauryn's time to open up and share her wisdom. She'd come a long way and learned a lot since the dark days that had followed *The Score*. Lauryn described the transformation that had occurred in her life to *Rolling Stone*: "There was a point where I had decided that I wasn't gonna pray anymore . . . because there were some things in my life that I knew weren't good for me. But I had decided that I needed those things. I knew that if I prayed, God would take them from me. So I was afraid. I was devastatingly terrified of prayer. And the moment I did pray, lo and behold, he removed all the negativity. Quicker than a snap. In the same speed, he loosened my tongue and a creative voice just came and wrote."

* * *

Part of Lauryn's truth-in-music crusade consisted of turning out a sound that could only be described as a visceral experience. When people listened to her album, she wanted them to feel her presence and her humanity with every fiber of their being. "I like the rawness of you being able to hear the scratch in the vocals," she explained in *Rolling Stone*. "I don't even want that taken away . . . because I was raised on music that was recorded before technology advanced to the place where it could be smooth. I wanna hear that thickness of sound. You can't get that from a computer, because a computer is too perfect. But the human element, that's what makes the hair on the back of my neck stand up."

Following this line of thought, she decided to rely exclusively on live musical instruments. The Fugees had also made extensive use of live instrumentation, but Lauryn was ready to go one step further by minimizing the use of samples and computer generated sounds. The move was all but unheard of in hip-hop. But Lauryn wasn't attempting to conform to hip-hop; she meant to build upon it. In the last months of 1997, she began recording in New York and, as she told *Entertainment Weekly*, "The first day in the studio, I think I ordered every instrument I ever fell in love with: harps, strings, timpani drums, organ, clarinets. . . ."

With the freedom to write, arrange, and produce her own album, it seemed that Lauryn's war for equality in the male-dominated music biz had been won. Alas, the war between the sexes still had some fire in it and would rage on in the studio. While none of the session players, programmers, and engineers working with Lauryn had the chutzpah to challenge the boss, she couldn't help noticing the different dynamic brought about by a female leader. "Men have a hard time taking direction from women, but when you pay somebody, you pay them to get it right," Lauryn told *Billboard*. "I think that women will be called 'bitches' and 'hard to work with' if they ask for and get what they want."

One thing that a woman would never be called, however, was a genius. The injustice of the double standard had been plaguing Lauryn since she first entered the spotlight with the Fugees. After *The Carnival* was released, the haste with which the public jumped to the conclusion that Wyclef had engineered all of Lauryn's success also hammered the point home. "This is a very sexist industry," she told *Essence*. "They will never throw the 'genius' title to a sister. They'll just call her diva and think it's a compliment. It's like our flair and vanity are put before our musical and intellectual contributions."

Of course, anyone who collaborated with Lauryn soon learned that she was in no way out of her depth. She described the initial sessions to *Rolling Stone*: "It's not easy for a woman to be in charge, because there's not that initial respect, and plus, there's a certain intuitive language that I speak that unless you know me, you probably won't understand right away. But the older musicians, especially, often knew exactly what I was talking about and gave me the voicing or chord I was looking for."

Making it clear that she intended to stay the course, Lauryn gained the admiration and respect of her coworkers. She could easily have chosen to take the path of least resistance by hiring powerful producers to do the work for her, but shirking responsibility had never been her style. "You know, it was quite a task," she told MTV of the recording process, "but something I definitely felt I was ready for and needed to do."

Not all of Lauryn's colleagues, however, were as helpful as she would have liked. Thus, not all of Lauryn's album was cut on the East Coast. "When I started recording in New York and New Jersey," she told *Rolling Stone*, "lots of people were talking to me about going different routes. I could feel people in my face, and I was picking up on bad vibes. I wanted a place where there was good vibes, where I was among family. And it was Tuff Gong."

Located on 56 Hope Road, within the lush landscape of Kingston, Jamaica, Tuff Gong had been Bob Marley's home and recording studio. It still housed many remaining members of the Marley clan. As Rohan's mate and the mother of a Marley grandchild, Lauryn Hill was now a part of that exclusive fraternity. Long before she ever met her boyfriend, Lauryn had felt an affinity for the Tuff Gong atmosphere. Back when *The Score* had just been released, she'd likened the Fugees' Booga Basement operation to Bob Marley's stronghold, telling Sony that the group had "always related to Tuff Gong."

In Kingston, the album came together piece by piece, just as Lauryn knew that it would from the very first moment of her arrival. Her engineer, "Commissioner Gordon" Williams, told *Rolling Stone* about their first morning at Tuff Gong. "Lauryn was in the living room next to the studio with about fifteen Marley grandchildren around her—the children of Stephen and Ziggy and Julian," he recalled, "and she starts singing this rap verse, and all the kids are repeating the last word of each line, chiming in very spontaneously because they were so into the song." As it turns out, the song she was rapping was none other than "Lost Ones," the very ditty that opens *The Miseducation of Lauryn Hill*.

After a few exceedingly fruitful months in Jamaica, Lauryn returned to her family in South Orange. Getting away from the New York pressure cooker had been a master stroke, allowing her to cement her ideas for the album's structure. With a solid foundation upon which to build, the Big Apple's bad vibes no longer posed a threat to the twenty-two-year-old solo artist.

The CD, however, was still a long way from completion. Many of the tracks had yet to be laid, and the mixing was nowhere near finalized. There were a few months' more work, easy—especially considering that Lauryn had yet to incorporate her guest stars into the album cuts. She may not have cared for top-of-the-line producers, but she was thrilled to use the album as a means of collaborating with some of her musically gifted friends, such as Mary J. Blige and D'Angelo.

Lauryn asked Blige to come in and sing on "I Used to Love Him," because, as she put it, "Mary sings from her heart." To record the stirring duet "Nothing Even Matters," Lauryn brought in neo-soul sensation D'Angelo. The two had become friends while sharing the bill on the Smokin' Grooves tour back in the summer of 1996. For her purposes, no one but D'Angelo would do. "I wanted to make a love song à la Roberta Flack and Donny Hathaway, and give people a humanistic approach to love again without all the physicality and overt sexuality," she told *Ebony*. "I wanted it to be about what it's like when your back starts to tingle and your stomach feels funny."

* * *

148

While all the songs on the album were deeply personal, the one that held the most meaning for Lauryn was "To Zion." Written about the birth of her son and the circumstances surrounding her pregnancy, the song was an ode to love and motherhood. Playing on the biblical significance of the name Zion, she told *Rolling Stone*, "I wanted it to be a revolutionary song about a spiritual movement, and also about my spiritual change, going from one place to another because of my son."

While Lauryn had written all the lyrics for the track, the instrumentation was provided by programmer Ché Guevara. "I had already done the song, and when she heard the song, she was like, 'This is it,' " Guevara told Sonic Net. Flamenco guitar had been worked into the song, and Guevara had some ideas as to whom Lauryn should use. His plans went straight out the window when he heard what Lauryn had in mind. She meant to ask none other than Carlos Santana, legendary guitar god and Rock 'n' Roll Hall of Famer, to appear on the song. "I was excited when she mentioned it," he recalled. "That's the kind of opportunity that you don't want to miss."

All that was left to do was send Santana the demo and hope for the best. The guitarist's answer was not long in the coming. "When I heard the song, it broke me up," Santana told *Entertainment Weekly*. "Especially when she says that the whole world is telling her, 'Man, what are you doing getting pregnant? You're at the peak of the game! You're at the peak of your career!' The world says you should be doing this, and the record company says you should be doing this. But your heart says, 'Go this way,' so you go that way. It takes a lot of courage to do that."

While Lauryn had tried her best to keep calm while awaiting Carlos Santana's reply, she could not hide her elation upon hearing the good news. This was, after all, the man whose record had opened her mind to the potential of music when she was just a child of five. Her admiration for his genius had not waned. "He plays guitar like a soul singer sings," she marveled to *Ebony*.

In the end, "To Zion" turned out to be the track that gave Lauryn the greatest sense of pride. Self-revealing and thought provoking, the tune epitomized the philosophy on songwriting that Lauryn had professed to *Rolling Stone*: "I don't feel like I have to put up a front to the people who want to hear my music. I don't want to write about things that separate me from the audience." Her album wasn't an excuse to flaunt her success or celebrate her stardom—rather, it was about exposing her pain, her joy, and her soul. In short, it was about being human.

Chapter Nine

Queen of the Hill

Eight months had passed since Lauryn first entered the studio to record *The Miseducation of Lauryn Hill*. In June 1998, it was all over. She could finally close the door on that chapter of her life without an ounce of regret, for she'd accomplished what she'd set out to do. Lauryn had repeatedly gone over each track, and her critical ear was satisfied at long last.

The time she had spent in the studio, however, was not without its distractions. Midway through her album, Lauryn had learned that she was pregnant again. This conception was met with a considerably livelier response than the last one. Despite her ceaseless work schedule, experience had shown that she didn't have to choose between a baby and her career. While Lauryn made every effort to spend as much time as possible with Zion, she trusted Rohan's fatherly instincts implicitly. In no uncertain terms, she told *Details* in the fall of 1998 that "we're together and we're raising a family. I don't consider myself a single mother at all."

Nonetheless, some sacrifices would have to be made. The most significant was passing up a leading role in Oprah Winfrey's and Jonathan Demme's adaptation of Tony Morrison's *Beloved*. Turning down one of the media's most powerful people and a highly acclaimed director all in one fell swoop couldn't have been easy, but such were Lauryn's priorities. "I was busy with Zion and diapers at the time," she told Planet Sound with only a hint of disappointment.

Still as interested in movies as ever, Lauryn had started her own production company, Black Market Films, to "push the envelope of merging music and movies." With an eye toward writing and directing a feature film, she hoped to get back into acting in order to learn the ropes. Unfortunately, important projects such as *Beloved* don't come around every month. "I get sent a lot of scripts," she told Planet Sound, "but it's always like 'She's twenty-two, she lives in New Jersey, she's a rapper. . . .' C'mon, I live that role every day!"

While many producers would have loved to attach the superstar to their films, Lauryn wasn't about to devote months of her life to anything less than brilliant. She passed on quite a few lucrative offers, including a screen adaptation of John Irving's *The Cider House*

Rules. "I want to treat films the same way I treat music," she explained to *Ebony*, "and not just do it for the sake of doing it. I'd like to do something new and original."

That certain something finally arrived in the form of a script for *Dreamgirls*. Joel Schumacher—the celebrated director of such hits as *St. Elmo's Fire*, *Falling Down*, two Batman installments, and most recently *8mm*—was interested in casting Lauryn as his leading lady. The Warner Bros. film, based on the hit Broadway play of the same name, would center on the life and times of a famous girl-group à la the Supremes. "Lauryn Hill is a world-class beauty," Schumacher declared in *Movieline*, "and she's also so smart."

After hearing Lauryn read for the part, the smitten director was even more effusive. "Some people are born stars," he told *Entertainment Weekly*. "Only God can make a tree, and only God could make Lauryn Hill. If I've admired her from afar, now I'm obsessed with her. I'll stalk her to the ends of the earth."

Production on the film was set to begin in March 1999. The timing would require Lauryn to shift around her tour dates. But if it meant playing Deena Jones, the Diana Ross character in *Dreamgirls*, she was ready to compromise.

While Lauryn was already a viable leading lady, time had yet to tell whether the same could be said of her as a solo artist. Although *The Miseducation of Lauryn Hill* was not scheduled for release until the last week of August 1998, the mood at Ruffhouse Records turned festive as soon as Lauryn presented her album. Ruffhouse CEO Chris Swartz had been the Fugee femme's earliest supporter, telling CNN that "we have the solo record on Lauryn Hill that we're very excited about" back in the first months of 1998. He was even more certain of future success when he spoke to the *Los Angeles Times* on the eve of *Miseducation*'s release, some seven months later: "I think when this new album comes out, she's really going to get her due as an artist."

Once the rest of the Ruffhouse and Columbia and Sony label executives had heard the record, they busied themselves with pats on the back as visions of dollar signs danced in their heads. Not fools, the execs were eager to get behind the star who was expected by one and all to rise highest and shine brightest.

Lauryn, on the other hand, still harbored some doubts. Years in the music business had taught her that sometimes a hype job is just a hype job. And while she felt that her album was beyond artistic reproach, there was no way of telling how its quality would translate into sales. She expressed her primary concern to *Ebony*, saying, "I think the only anxiety that I felt was . . . that once you release something, it's a reflection of you, and people will beat up on it."

By working overtime in the recording studio, Lauryn knew that she'd done all she could to eliminate the chance of such an outcome. After the album left her hands, Lauryn had to decide on the single that would introduce her work to the public. According to programmer Ché Guevara, Lauryn "wanted to lead it off with something happy and 'Doo Wop' was the only happy song she had on the album."

In July, Lauryn set out to film the video for "Doo Wop (That Thing)." Filmed in Manhattan's Washington Heights, the video shows two Lauryns singing side by side at a block party. On the left side of the split screen, she is done up in full 1967 regalia, complete with a wig and zebra-striped dress, to pay respect to old-school R&B and doo-wop. The right side features the present-day Lauryn Hill in an homage to hip-hop culture. The message is simply that the more things change, the more they stay the same.

Already six months pregnant, she took special pains to hide her girth during the six-day shoot. Lauryn managed to accomplish this considerable feat by choosing two of the most figure-friendly ensembles she could find and making good use of camera angles. Those who weren't in the know were none the wiser after viewing the bright and vivacious video.

Released in late August 1998, *The Miseducation of Lauryn Hill* was an immediate hit. The album was acquired by approximately 420,000 Americans in the first week alone. The number was high enough to eclipse the record previously set by Madonna's *Ray of Light* for selling more copies in one week than any other female solo artist. Needless to add, the record entered the *Billboard* pop chart at Number 1.

Slashing through gender and color lines, Lauryn's solo album became a universal favorite and was generally acknowledged as a milestone in music history. Despite what some critics called her "preachy" manner, it seemed that everybody liked Lauryn Hill. "In New York, I've had Italian cops come up to me at the Port Authority [bus station] and tell me they love the record," she told *Spin*. "I think the world is a lot smaller than I thought [it was] growing up."

No sooner had the album been released than *Time* magazine labeled it "Hip-Hop's Number One CD," describing it as "intelligent and essential." A few months later, music critics all over the United States found common ground by naming *Miseducation* the Album of the Year. *Spin* magazine was in a state of bliss, citing Lauryn's "sing-song melodies, edgy production, enviable rhyme skills, back-to-church vocals" and her "almost unnerving perfection." *Rolling Stone* called the album a "savvy mix of live instrumentation and electronic innovation, early-Seventies songcraft and late-Nineties beats, liquid rapping and sanctified singing." *Entertainment Weekly* also bestowed the Album of the Year honor, characterizing it as "one of the most forceful statements ever by a woman in pop."

Week after week, music chart watchers could expect to find *Miseducation* perched within the Top 5. By year's end, *Miseducation* had gone triple platinum and Lauryn was being hailed as a latter-day Aretha Franklin. Her name was on the tip of every tongue, and each time "Doo Wop" came wafting through the radio, people couldn't help expressing their admiration. But where exactly was Lauryn while all this was going on?

In her parents' New Jersey home, where else? With the baby due any day, Lauryn had holed up with her family, telling *Entertainment Weekly*, "I'm big and fat, so I'm not really doing anything." She'd done more than enough already. In the past year, she'd penned and produced tracks for CeCe Winans and Aretha Franklin, two of her childhood idols. (Actually, make that three—she'd also found time to work with role model Whitney Houston.) Under the auspices of the Refugee Project, she'd sent a group of underprivileged kids to camp in the

Catskill Mountains. Add to that the countless photo shoots, interviews, awards ceremonies, and press conferences, and you end up with one young woman badly in need of some peace and quiet. The final weeks of her pregnancy found Lauryn enjoying exactly that.

She could finally sit back and savor all the love being sent in her direction. No longer worried about some destructive love affair or her group mates' reaction to her fame, her joy was undiluted. She'd gone from listening to classics to creating them—and it felt good. "I was listening to Nina Simone and Stevie Wonder records back in the day and feeling 'Oh, God!' and wanting to cry," she recalled in *Entertainment Weekly*. "So when you have people telling you 'This made me cry' or 'Girl, you wrote that song for me,' it makes me feel like I'm moving in the right direction. Beyond what the critics say. Beyond what the industry says. What the people say."

Even in the sunniest of latitudes, a little rain must fall. Lauryn's shiny, happy existence was not exempt from this general rule. Witness her chart-topping album, itself full of sad verse and tragic inspiration. "During this album," she told *Rolling Stone*, "I turned to the Bible and wrote songs that I drew comfort from, because I lost my grandmother, my cousin, a seven-year-old friend—a lot of people close to me." *The Miseducation of Lauryn Hill* would be dedicated to the memory of her dearly departed family and friends.

The creation of a monster hit album and the adulation of millions is hardly a guarantee of carefree living. The first cloud to darken Lauryn's bright horizon was the termination of the *Dreamgirls* project in September 1998. To her dismay, Warner Bros. put the kibosh on the film, and with it, the role Lauryn seemed born to play. Director Joel Schumacher was crestfallen. "It's a big disappointment," he told *Movieline*. "When David Geffen called me up two years ago and asked, 'Would you direct *Dreamgirls* for me?' it seemed like a dream come true. I leapt into it and have spent the last two years preparing it. I still don't know what happened, but as far as I know right now, it's cancelled."

So Lauryn went back to the drawing board, going through the pile of scripts collecting dust in her South Orange home. When asked about a possible role in the *Mission: Impossible* sequel by *Entertainment Weekly*, Lauryn would only say, "There are some things, but nothing I will sign any pen to paper yet."

To add to Lauryn's concerns, there was more of the dismaying talk of the friction between her, Wyclef, and Pras. Granted, the rumors were sparked by lyrics that Lauryn herself had penned for *Miseducation*. Songs such as "Lost Ones," "Superstar," and "Ex-Factor" gave many a listener that "nudge, nudge, wink, wink" feeling. Lauryn's less-informed acolytes were quick to translate her general condemnation of the music industry into a personal slur against Clef and Pras.

Arguing that none of her songs, save perhaps "Ex-Factor," were about any one person in particular, Lauryn vociferously denied having dissed her homies through song. Although they hadn't spoken to each other in months, the Fugees were still together. Despite the solo careers of all three members (after his successful "Ghetto Superstar" single from the *Bulworth* soundtrack, Pras had put out an album of the same name), their plans to reunite were alive and well. While the date of this reunion had yet to be determined, press statements made by Wyclef, Pras, and Lauryn dispelled any notion of an imminent splintering. "The deal is," Lauryn told *Girl* magazine, "we definitely need to get back together, sit in the studio, and create. We need to talk about life—our personal lives, our individual lives—and just bug out. . . . It's going to be interesting to hear what that music sounds like when we get together."

Further proof of the "mo' money, mo' problems" theory came in the way of a legal dispute that threatened to mar Lauryn's credibility forever. The four members of New Ark group whom she had hired to work on her record—Vada Nobles, Rasheem Pugh, Tejumold Newton, and Johari Newton—had been in contact with Ruffhouse Records' attorneys since *Miseducation*'s debut. In November 1998, they filed a lawsuit alleging that they had not received the proper songwriting and production credits for their contribution to the album. Lauryn had, indeed, credited them for their work on four of her songs, yet the group professed to have had a hand in nine more.

Specifically, New Ark demanded they be recognized as the principal writers of "Every Ghetto, Every City" and "Everything Is Everything," and as major or partial contributors to eleven other songs. Even Lauryn's work on Aretha's "A Rose Is Still a Rose" was brought under scrutiny, as the group claimed that they had not received their rightful credit on Franklin's album. All told, they wanted a multi-million dollar settlement, equal to one-third of the royalties generated by *The Miseducation of Lauryn Hill* in its first three months of release.

The tale they told painted a rather sinister portrait of Lauryn. New Ark's side of the story goes as follows: When planning her solo album back in 1997, Lauryn had called her friend of four years, Rasheem Pugh, whom she knew to be a part of New Ark. After she promised to credit and pay the group for major contributions to the album, they set to work, thinking this would be their big break. While no contract was ever signed, the four musicians took Lauryn's word at face value and spent months collaborating with her in her home studio. Finally, Lauryn followed the counsel of her advisers and violated the verbal agreement.

"She is not a musician, she is not a producer," New Ark's lawyer declared. "[New Ark] will make another album and everyone will see that they were the ones responsible for this album. I dare say if you put Lauryn Hill in a studio alone, she couldn't do it again. Album No. 2 for her is not going to sound like this."

Such characterization is hardly in keeping with the generous face that Lauryn has presented to the world since before she was a superstar. This was, after all, the same young woman who started a breakfast program at her high school and who was now spending her free time trying to help inner-city kids. Could she really be capable of such a dastardly deed?

Lauryn's friends and business associates didn't think so. "Lauryn is a very gifted arranger, producer and writer, as well as a vocalist; she's the whole package," said *Miseducation*'s sound engineer Gordon Williams. "It's definitely her vision." The official statement from the Hill camp was that Lauryn felt "deeply betrayed" because New Ark had been "appropriately credited for their contribution on the album. This is an attempt to take advantage of her success, and it will be dealt with through the courts."

While the jury is still out, one has to wonder whether this "your word against mine" lawsuit is just another example of the music industry's sexism. Months before the litigation surfaced, Lauryn was discussing her plight as a female in hip-hop with *Horizon Magazine*. "It's a really silly battle to have to fight, because it's all in the name of making good music."

Whatever the outcome, suffice it to say that royalty suits, despite being a very common problem in the recording biz, are never as cut and dried as either the plaintiffs or the defendants make them out to be. In any collaborative process, there are bound to be people who either believe that their idea was stolen or are convinced that they are the parents of someone else's brainchild. According to Grammy-winning songwriter and producer Glen Ballard's explanation in the *Los Angeles Times*, the songwriting process is much like "a group of people with their hands on a Ouija board: Who's moving the thing? We all are, I guess. At the end of the day, music is a collaborative medium. . . . When it comes to pinning down who did what, a lot of that gets lost in the process."

* * *

On November 12, 1998, an event took place that overshadowed any negativity surrounding the business sector of Lauryn's life. Not even the acrimonious lawsuit could dampen her spirits after the birth of her daughter, Selah Louise. In a family that valued one another over anything else in the world, the baby's arrival was met with all the fanfare of a ticker-tape parade.

Unlike the rambunctious Zion, Lauryn's daughter was the epitome of tranquility. Selah's quiet infancy was music to her parents' ears. "From the moment she was born," Lauryn told *Teen People*, "I could see how different her personality was from my son's. She's so sweet and peaceful."

Zion was already old enough to rap, using everything from Lauryn's microphone to her bottles of nail polish as his MC props. All this familial commotion was still transpiring in South Orange, a place where Lauryn has vowed to remain. "I have everything I need here," she said. "I love my home, I loved growing up there and I will raise my children there."

Amid the flurry of activity ushered in by the newborn, Lauryn was also called upon to resume the glamorous duties of stardom. Crowding her plate were plans for an upcoming U.S. tour, a video shoot for her second single, "Ex-Factor," a musical guest appearance on *Sat-*

urday Night Live, and a performance at the Billboard Music Awards where she was nominated in multiple categories.

Balancing the demands of motherhood with fame was not easy. Lauryn would have to be as inventive in her personal life as she was in the studio, if she wanted to succeed at her dual role. "I don't want [Zion and Selah] to feel like they miss Mommy. So I challenge myself to make sure I'm with them as much as possible," she told *Rolling Stone*. "Raising children is a twenty-four-hour job, and makin' music is a twenty-four-hour job, so I have to be really careful how I do things."

Part of her responsibility lay in being a good role model for her children and, by extension, the world at large. Lauryn's commitment to her value system was soon tested by, of all things, her December 5 performance on *Saturday Night Live*. Aside from doing her act, the *SNL* team also offered her a chance to appear in a sketch. As she looked through the script, her heart sank. She was being asked to play a ho in a skit titled "Pimp Chat." If she didn't like the street-walker shtick, *SNL* was willing to let her play a female pimp.

Lauryn didn't need to think very long before nixing both propositions. No way was she going to spit in the face of her songs' messages by perpetuating negative stereotypes. Not about to sell her soul for a few extra minutes of airtime on *Saturday Night Live*, Lauryn limited her participation to the music segment. The day after her performance, she was off to Las Vegas where she was scheduled to perform "Doo Wop" at the 1998 Billboard Music Awards. Broadcast live on Fox, the awards ceremony provided Lauryn with another opportunity to showcase her talents for an audience of millions. Better still, the organization presented her with the R&B Album of the Year award.

The *SNL* telecast and the Billboard Music Awards were Lauryn's first live performances since the release of *Miseducation* over three months earlier. The album had just begun to slide down the chart when the added exposure kicked it right back up into big business. The CD again hovered close to *Billboard*'s coveted Number 1 slot. Lauryn herself had a hard time believing that a retro-soul/R&B/hip-hop record could hold down a Top 10 chart position for this long. "To know that people have responded in such a way," she told *Spin*, "makes me realize that they're actually very ready for truth and real experiences."

The success of Lauryn's album made Grammy nominations all but inevitable. Here was a record that the world could agree on. People with vastly different backgrounds and musical tastes could actually groove to the same rhythm if *Miseducation* was in the CD player. What Lauryn had accomplished was a rare feat, and no one was too surprised when the Grammy nominations were announced on January 5, 1999.

The young recording artist was honored with no less than a precedent-setting ten nominations: two for Best R&B Song ("Doo Wop" and "A Rose Is Still a Rose"), Best Rap Solo Performance ("Lost Ones"), Best Duo or Group R&B Performance ("Nothing Even Matters" with D'Angelo), Best Female Pop Vocal Performance ("Can't Take My Eyes Off of You"), Best Female R&B Vocal Performance ("Doo Wop"), Best R&B Album, Producer of the Year—Nonclassical, Best New Artist, and finally, Album of the Year. In the forty-one-year history of the Grammy awards, no female performer had ever received so many nominations.

Amazingly, the late-breaking news was overshadowed by another event taking place within the Hill clan. Malaney, Lauryn's older brother, was becoming a father. By an odd coincidence, Malaney's girlfriend was in labor just as the Grammy nominations were handed out. The whole of the Hill family, save Lauryn and Rohan, were at the hospital presiding over the birth. "Of course, the baby is more joyous," close friend of the family Miriam Farrakhan told the Newark *Star-Ledger*. "The baby is a blessing."

Far from feeling upstaged by her new nephew, Lauryn wouldn't have had the baby arrive at any other time. As hip-hop music's reigning "It Girl," she knew that only the miracle of birth could bring her back down to earth. "I was really happy with the nominations," she told *Teen People*, "but my brother's girlfriend had been in labor for twenty-eight hours that day. Just at the time when I could have gotten so big-headed, I had something so beautiful and humbling to focus on."

As reporters eager to hear how Lauryn felt about her record-breaking nominations gathered on the well-manicured lawn of Valerie and Mal's South Orange home, Rohan came out to greet them. He had a message from Lauryn. Explaining that Lauryn was tending to their baby upstairs, he told the press that she "gives thanks to all the people. And God's grace and blessing to everyone. And she gives thanks to the Father."

Perhaps little Selah's feedings and diaper changes weren't the only reasons behind Lauryn's inability to face the press. Could it be that the cool, calm, and collected superstar needed more than a moment to regain her composure? Describing her state of mind, Rohan told the *Star-Ledger* that "I don't think surprised is the right word. She is elated. And appreciative of the people, who feel for her the way she feels for them. It's a reciprocal love, y'know. It's a oneness."

Chapter Ten

A League of Her Own

The deluge of Grammy nominations only reinforced many music critics' belief that Lauryn Hill had single-handedly rescued hip-hop. The mainstream media seemed to agree, spreading the word of Lauryn's heroics throughout the land. There was even a noticeable rise in hip-hop-related articles after Lauryn's overwhelming commercial success. The catalyst herself would soon grow tired of her own likeness—seeing it plastered all over the covers of magazines such as *Details*, *Rolling Stone*, *Teen People*, and even the revered *Time*.

With a month to go until the Grammys, the whole country seemed to be placing their bets on Lauryn to win. While she already felt like the most blessed person this side of the Milky Way, she didn't find out how lucky she truly was until about five days after the Grammy nominations were announced. Providence intervened when Lauryn least expected—while she was rehearsing for her upcoming tour.

The Lauryn Hill Story

On January 10, 1999, she was in Manhattan running through some steps for the tour that was scheduled to kick off in Tokyo come January 21. As the rehearsal wound down, Rohan volunteered to go outside and warm up their car. The hour was late and he was tired. While awaiting Lauryn's exit, he fell asleep in the car. As he slept, an unspecified electrical malfunction sparked an engine fire. Rohan woke up to find the hood of his car in flames and himself engulfed by dangerous smoke. He tried to open the doors, but they wouldn't unlock, and the automatic windows would not budge. He was trapped within the burning car.

But for the grace of God, Rohan would surely have perished in the fire. As it turned out, however, two passing policemen noticed the blaze. Fortunately, they also caught sight of Rohan's hands on the car window. They jumped to his rescue, shattering the driver's-side window and forcing the door open. That's when Lauryn came rushing out of the building. Seeing the car on fire, she thought the worst. "She was hysterical," said Officer Jose Segura, who had pulled Rohan from the flames. "She thought he was still in the car."

Miraculously, aside from a nasty case of smoke inhalation, Rohan emerged unscathed. After a brief visit to the hospital, he was shepherded back to the South Orange homestead, safe and sound. "He's comfortable," Lauryn's spokesperson told the *New York Daily News*. "But, you know—it's scary. He'll probably be going to a physical today or tomorrow, just to make sure that everything is fine. This was just great luck."

And didn't Lauryn know it. For the short period of time she'd believed Rohan to be injured or worse, her life had stopped dead. The experience had been one of the most agonizing she'd ever known. There wasn't a doubt in her mind that his salvation was a gift from God. "Once again, I think that God is so great," she told *Teen People*, "because Rohan came out without a scratch."

The certainty that God was on her side had long fortified Lauryn. Hers has always been a spirituality that went beyond mere words and publicity posturing. Its positive influence could be felt in each and every move she made. Simply put, she's a good person—always has been. She's made good things happen for others as well as for herself. And she has received her just rewards: The day after Rohan's close call, for example, she was presented with the American Music Award for Favorite New Soul/R&B Artist.

Lauryn's first-ever solo tour began as scheduled, in Tokyo's Nippon Budokan Hall on January 21. Her star shone just as brightly in Japan as it did in the States. *Miseducation* had gone platinum in Japan and many of the country's denizens turned out to see her sold-out shows. Lauryn's larger-than-life performance ensured that her fans would get exactly what they bargained for, if not more.

Traveling with an orchestra of thirteen to eighteen musicians, Lauryn had every intention of putting on a grand spectacle. Despite never having been on tour without the Fugees, she made her way through the set with nary a sign of struggle. At the end of the show, however, she was both drained and invigorated. It couldn't have been easy for her. In years past, she'd always had Wyclef or Pras to pick up the slack. Now the full responsibility rested on her narrow shoulders. But she had done it. People flocked to see her first solo concert, and they walked away satisfied.

The three shows in Tokyo were followed by a one-night stint in Osaka. Then, after a brief respite, she was due to perform in London's prestigious 4,000-seat Brixton Academy, on Friday, February 5. None of this was new territory for Lauryn, who'd already traveled the world with the Fugees. Yet there were some differences.

Not only were these her first performances as a solo artist, but this was also her first tour since she'd become a mother. The eighteen months that she'd been away from the Fugees had been full of change and growth, both in her career and her personal life. Now going on twenty-four, Lauryn had accomplished more than she ever thought possible. Even her mom was reeling from Lauryn's overwhelming success. "Frankly," she told *Entertainment Weekly*, Lauryn's accomplishments "often leave me at a loss for words—and as an English teacher I'm not supposed to be at a loss for words."

As a mother of two young kids, Lauryn was adamant about spending quality time whenever her schedule permitted. Going to London presented the perfect opportunity. Lauryn arrived in London with Rohan, Valerie, Zion, and Selah in tow. This trip would not be like the others. She'd already been through the plane-to-hotel-to-concert wringer. It was time to stop the insanity and see the sights. "This is my fifth time in London," she explained to the *Independent*, "but it's the first time I've been able to enjoy myself. I'm here with my whole family and the vibe is awesome."

Just as everyone expected, Lauryn's sold-out London show provided her British fans with a jolly good time, as well as garnered a round of applause from the local press syndicates. The *Daily Telegraph* even went so far as to declare, "If Bob Marley's 1975 show at London's Lyceum—with its famed 'No Woman No Cry'—was the pop pinnacle of its decade, then this may have been its Nineties equivalent."

But Friday's concert would not be the last

London saw of Lauryn Hill. A Saturday press conference at the Sony Café would be followed by a special Saturday night performance for contest winners, and the BBC cameras captured the whole soiree on tape for a Valentine's Day special.

Through it all, Selah and Zion remained either at their mother's side or watching from the wings. Although they cried for the duration of the British press conference, they were surely smiling soon after. As Lauryn told the *Independent*, "Zion went to the zoo and we went kinda crazy . . . we have to ship Zion's toys home because we don't have room in the plane."

Despite her frequent job-related absences, worldwide success has actually made Lauryn a more careful and thoughtful mother. Like any other parent, her children's education is a major concern. "People suggest home or private school," she told *Ebony*, "but I don't want to alienate my son. I want him to be exposed to everything. I want him to go abroad, to see that the world is a lot bigger than five blocks. I want him to have a regular childhood."

Granted, most kids don't go on the road with their parents before they're old enough to walk. But then again, most kids aren't the scions of a musical dynasty. Lauryn's U.S. tour began at Detroit's Fox Theatre on February 18, and Selah and Zion were right there with Lauryn and Rohan. This fact alone is revealing: Any tour that includes a specially equipped "baby bus" can't possibly include the sex, drugs, and rock 'n' roll that are often the staples of life on the road.

Suburbia, nightly feedings, and back-to-school shopping sprees will certainly help keep Lauryn's life in perspective. But Lauryn has no intention of turning "matronly." Abhorring the dowdy image associated with being a mom, she wouldn't even allow any below-the-shoulder pictures to be taken of her while she was in the late stages of her pregnancy with Selah. After Selah's birth, however, it was a different story.

The provocative images of the newly lithe beauty communicated Lauryn's message loud and clear. Sure, they seemed to say, she has kids and, make no mistake, she loves them to death, but she's not reaching for the Geritol just yet. Lauryn is a young, vital twenty-three-year-old woman. And she's going to make sure no one forgets it. As she told *Vibe*, "I never wanted to be perceived as not being sexy or as being matronly."

At heart, the superwoman remains a girl. She's still best friends with her mother, she still loves nice clothes and insists on looking pretty, and she still lives at home. In light of all she's done, is there anything wrong with that?

* * *

After launching the tour in Detroit, team Hill made its way to Chicago. From there, it was on to St. Louis. With her sights set squarely on the biggest industry event of the year, Lauryn had arranged for a three-day break after the St. Louis show. February 23, 24, and 25 would be reserved for preparing for, participating in, and recuperating from the event in which the music industry congratulates its own on a job well done—the Grammy Awards.

Held in L.A.'s voluminous Shrine Auditorium on Wednesday, February 24, the Grammy Awards would see hundreds of stars turn out to face the ceaselessly flashing cameras. Here, hip-hop, rock, pop, country, folk, classical, blues, jazz, and R&B musicians come together, in all their finery, to see and be seen.

Lauryn's was the success story of the night, perhaps the decade. Her mind-boggling ten nominations had celebs and fans alike wondering how many would be parlayed into the coveted trophies. Would she win for Album of the Year? Or would the catch go to one of the other ladies in the house: Madonna, Shania Twain, or Garbage's Shirley Manson? Upsets had been known to happen and, considering that the NARAS had always treated hip-hop like the music industry's dirty little secret, Lauryn, for one, wasn't about to start counting her trophies until the seals on all the envelopes had been broken.

Lauryn receiving a record-breaking ten nominations wasn't the only first for women in music that night. For Lilith Fair devotees everywhere, the evening of the forty-first Grammy Awards took on all the significance of a "Take Back the Night" rally. This year, the most illustrious category of all, Album of the Year, had nothing but female candidates. Lauryn's jackpot and the dominance of female recording artists in general lent a heightened air of expectation to the affair.

For the woman at the center of the hoopla, the widely watched event portended great things. Not only did she stand a chance of winning for Album of the Year and seeing her sales figures climb as a result, but she was also set to perform one of her album tracks before an audience of millions. While she had initially intended to use the opportunity to debut her latest single, "Ex-Factor," all plans were scrapped when Carlos Santana agreed to join her onstage.

Santana's guitar virtuosity was so vital to the faithful rendering of "To Zion" that the thought of performing it without him hadn't even crossed Lauryn's mind. "That was a song that I'd never had the opportunity to perform [live]," she said, "and it was wonderful because Carlos Santana was available and I said, 'You know what, we gotta do "Zion." ' It was something for me, it was something for my child."

When reporters from MTV, E!, and *Entertainment Tonight* questioned the stars assembling outside the Shrine Auditorium on who they thought would win, they had much to say. The consensus was best stated by stalwart metal-head Rob Zombie. "I think there's two words: Lauryn Hill," he told MTV. "She'll win everything and we'll all go home and say, 'I knew it.'"

Since many of the awards are announced hours before the CBS broadcast begins, Lauryn was a three-time winner before much of the world had tuned in to watch. She had won for Best R&B Album, Best R&B Song for "Doo Wop," as well as Best Female R&B Vocal Performance for "Doo Wop." All in all, it was shaping up to be the biggest night of Lauryn's career.

Lauryn would watch several of her nominations translate into awards for other artists, but the honors that she was finally granted were worth the wait. Despite her nervous anticipation, she betrayed no sign of tension as presenters B. B. King and Eric Clapton rattled off the nominees for the year's Best New Artist. Only at the Grammys could Lauryn find herself in competition as diverse as the Dixie Chicks, the Backstreet Boys, Natalie Imbruglia, and Andrea Bocelli. How does one decide among artists as different as these?

To many people's satisfaction, the apples vs.

oranges situation was resolved in Lauryn's favor. Even before her name was called, a large contingent of the audience was vocally rooting for the young woman widely acknowledged to be the savior of hip-hop's soul. When B. B. King announced her the winner, everyone in the auditorium came to their feet. After kissing Rohan, Lauryn breezed up to the stage and accepted the trophy with words from Psalm 40. Bubbling over with gratitude, she thanked everyone from Rohan and the kids to Sony CEO Tommy Mottola. Her one-minute speech concluded with Lauryn saying, "God bless you. Stay positive, stay strong, one love y'all."

But the show was far from over. As the final performer of the night, Lauryn had plenty of time to change out of her red knit beret, rootsy sarong skirt, and white tank top. When her time came, the camera found her resplendent in a white ensemble that looked like it just came off the Milan runway. As the poignant strains of Santana's guitar broke the silence, Lauryn began telling her life with her song. Those lucky enough to have caught the exquisite performance understand why this particular songstress had been singled out for so many nominations. As record sales would soon show, anyone who had not been convinced by "Doo Wop" couldn't help being won over by Lauryn's soul-stirring execution of "To Zion."

As the light went down on Lauryn's act,

master of ceremonies Rosie O'Donnell brought an end to the suspense. It was time to announce the Album of the Year. A hush fell over the crowd as presenters Whitney Houston and Sting assumed their positions. After trading the usual quips, the two got down to business. Judging by the audience reaction, neither Sheryl Crow's *The Globe Sessions* (Best Rock Album) nor Madonna's *Ray of Light* (Best Pop Album)—not to mention Garbage's *Version 2.0* or Shania Twain's *Come on Over*—had what it took to topple the hands-down favorite, Lauryn's *The Miseducation of Lauryn Hill* (Best R&B Album).

Before her name was even announced, Lauryn's friend and sometime collaborator Whitney Houston was already jumping for joy and waving her fist in the air. As predicted, the Grammy for Album of the Year went to Lauryn—the first time the honor was bestowed upon a hip-hop artist. Having just performed, Lauryn emerged from backstage to accept the top honor of the night and the standing ovation accompanying it. The magnitude of the moment had clearly yet to sink in. "This is so amazing," she gasped, beaming. "This is crazy, because this is hip-hop music."

For all her life's struggles, hard work, and love of music to culminate in this historic moment meant more to Lauryn than she could ever express. While she thanked God as well as everyone who had helped with album, none of it expressed the full depth of the emotion she was feeling. "I feel crazy," she later effervesced to the press. "I don't even . . . I'm kind of in a zone right now. I feel very blessed. Who could ask for [this]? An album that I poured my heart and soul into, [and then] to see people receive it like this is a huge reward—I'm very thankful."

There was a lot to be thankful for. Aside from the satisfaction of being recognized for her talent, Lauryn's five Grammy wins set a new record for most Grammys won by a female in one year. She had surpassed the four-Grammy standard set by Carole King back in 1971, and record sales would soon reflect this landmark achievement. Just one week after the awards ceremony, the already robust sales of *Miseducation* had doubled. Since its debut six months prior, the album had gone platinum five times over, and it was once again Number 1 on the charts.

After one all-too-brief day of celebration, Lauryn returned to her tour. She left much of her family behind, but she found a hero's welcome waiting to embrace her at every stop. Lauryn had indeed become a hero, not only by virtue of her never-ending procession of awards—five Grammys, two from *Soul Train*, one from *Billboard*—but for the music that had earned them.

While Lauryn's tour bus would drive on until

her April 1 homecoming show in Newark, she would take a quick time-out in March to pay a visit to the ballroom of New York's historic Waldorf-Astoria hotel for the fourteenth annual Rock 'n' Roll Hall of Fame induction dinner.

Having been asked to induct the Staple Singers, performers of such spiritual seventies' hits as "I'll Take You There" and "Respect Yourself," into the Hall of Fame, Lauryn was proud to turn out for the fabled ceremony. Among the stars being honored that night were Paul McCartney, Curtis Mayfield, Bruce Springsteen, and Billy Joel. In the music industry, nothing says "life achievement award" quite like an induction into the Hall of Fame.

Dressed in red from head to toe, Lauryn gave an impassioned speech on behalf of the Staple Singers. Only fifteen short years ago, their soulful brand of rock 'n' roll had touched her heart and helped start her on the road to fame. As the well-heeled guests watched her deliver the induction address, many were impressed by the young woman who'd become a legend in her own time. After Lauryn finished her fiery oration, she welcomed the Staple Singers into the Rock 'n' Roll Hall of Fame, where, one day, she'll no doubt go on to join them.

Don't miss a single one of these outstanding biographies.

Published by Ballantine Books.
Available in your local bookstore.